Tucholsky   Wagner   Zola   Scott   Sydow   Freud   Schlegel
Turgenev   Wallace   Fonatne
Twain   Walther von der Vogelweide   Fouqué   Friedrich II. von Preußen
Weber   Freiligrath   Frey
Fechner   Fichte   Weiße Rose   von Fallersleben   Kant   Ernst   Frommel
Richthofen
Engels   Fielding   Hölderlin   Dumas
Fehrs   Faber   Flaubert   Eichendorff   Tacitus
Eliasberg   Ebner Eschenbach
Feuerbach   Maximilian I. von Habsburg   Fock   Zweig   Vergil
Ewald   Eliot
Goethe   London
Mendelssohn   Balzac   Shakespeare   Elisabeth von Österreich   Dostojewski   Ganghofer
Lichtenberg   Rathenau   Doyle   Gjellerup
Trackl   Stevenson   Hambruch
Mommsen   Tolstoi   Lenz   Droste-Hülshoff
Thoma   Hanrieder
Dach   von Arnim   Hägele   Humboldt
Verne   Hauff
Karrillon   Reuter   Rousseau   Hagen   Hauptmann   Gautier
Garschin
Damaschke   Defoe   Hebbel   Baudelaire
Descartes
Hegel   Kussmaul   Herder
Wolfram von Eschenbach   Dickens   Schopenhauer
Bronner   Darwin   Melville   Grimm   Jerome   Rilke   George
Campe   Horváth   Aristoteles   Bebel   Proust
Bismarck   Vigny   Barlach   Voltaire   Federer   Herodot
Gengenbach   Heine
Storm   Casanova   Tersteegen   Grillparzer   Georgy
Chamberlain   Lessing   Langbein   Gilm   Gryphius
Brentano   Lafontaine
Strachwitz   Claudius   Schiller   Kralik   Iffland   Sokrates
Katharina II. von Rußland   Bellamy   Schilling
Gerstäcker   Raabe   Gibbon   Tschechow
Löns   Hesse   Hoffmann   Gogol   Wilde   Gleim   Vulpius
Luther   Heym   Hofmannsthal   Morgenstern
Roth   Klee   Hölty   Goedicke
Luxemburg   Heyse   Klopstock   Kleist
Puschkin   Homer   Mörike
Machiavelli   La Roche   Horaz   Musil
Navarra   Aurel   Musset   Kierkegaard   Kraft   Kraus
Lamprecht   Kind   Moltke
Nestroy   Marie de France   Kirchhoff   Hugo
Laotse   Ipsen   Liebknecht
Nietzsche   Nansen   Ringelnatz
Marx   Lassalle   Gorki   Klett
von Ossietzky   Leibniz
May   vom Stein   Lawrence   Irving
Petalozzi   Knigge
Platon   Kafka
Sachs   Pückler   Michelangelo   Kock
Poe   Liebermann
de Sade   Praetorius   Mistral   Zetkin   Korolenko

The publishing house tredition has created the series **TREDITION CLASSICS**. It contains classical literature works from over two thousand years. Most of these titles have been out of print and off the bookstore shelves for decades.

The book series is intended to preserve the cultural legacy and to promote the timeless works of classical literature. As a reader of a **TREDITION CLASSICS** book, the reader supports the mission to save many of the amazing works of world literature from oblivion.

The symbol of **TREDITION CLASSICS** is Johannes Gutenberg (1400 – 1468), the inventor of movable type printing.

With the series, tredition intends to make thousands of international literature classics available in printed format again – worldwide.

All books are available at book retailers worldwide in paperback and in hardcover. For more information please visit: www.tredition.com

tredition was established in 2006 by Sandra Latusseck and Soenke Schulz. Based in Hamburg, Germany, tredition offers publishing solutions to authors and publishing houses, combined with worldwide distribution of printed and digital book content. tredition is uniquely positioned to enable authors and publishing houses to create books on their own terms and without conventional manufacturing risks.

For more information please visit: www.tredition.com

Letters to Sir William Windham and Mr. Pope

Henry St. John, Viscount Bolingbroke

Imprint

This book is part of the TREDITION CLASSICS series.

Author: Henry St. John, Viscount Bolingbroke
Cover design: toepferschumann, Berlin (Germany)

Publisher: tredition GmbH, Hamburg (Germany)
ISBN: 978-3-8495-0722-0

www.tredition.com
www.tredition.de

Copyright:
The content of this book is sourced from the public domain.

The intention of the TREDITION CLASSICS series is to make world literature in the public domain available in printed format. Literary enthusiasts and organizations worldwide have scanned and digitally edited the original texts. tredition has subsequently formatted and redesigned the content into a modern reading layout. Therefore, we cannot guarantee the exact reproduction of the original format of a particular historic edition. Please also note that no modifications have been made to the spelling, therefore it may differ from the orthography used today.

Contents

INTRODUCTION

Henry St. John, who became Viscount Bolingbroke in 1712, was born on the 1st of October, 1678, at the family manor of Battersea, then a country village. His grandfather, Sir Walter St. John, lived there with his wife Johanna, - daughter to Cromwell's Chief Justice, Oliver St. John, - in one home with the child's father, Henry St. John, who was married to the second daughter of Robert Rich, Earl of Warwick. The child's grandfather, a man of high character, lived to the age of eighty-seven; and his father, more a man of what is miscalled pleasure, to the age of ninety. It was chiefly by his grandfather and grandmother that the education of young Henry St. John was cared for. Simon Patrick, afterwards Bishop of Ely, was for some years a chaplain in their home. By his grandfather and grandmother the child's religious education may have been too formally cared for. A passage in Bolingbroke's letter to Pope shows that he was required as a child to read works of a divine who "made a hundred and nineteen sermons on the hundred and nineteenth Psalm."

After education at Eton and Christchurch, Henry St. John travelled abroad, and in the year 1700 he married, at the age of twenty-two, Frances, daughter and co-heiress of Sir Henry Winchescomb, a Berkshire baronet. She had much property, and more in prospect.

In the year 1701, Henry St. John entered Parliament as member for Wotton Bassett, the family borough. He acted with the Tories, and became intimate with their leader, Robert Harley. He soon became distinguished as the ablest and most vigorous of the young supporters of the Tory party. He was a handsome man and a brilliant speaker, delighted in by politicians who, according to his own image in the Letter to Windham, "grow, like hounds, fond of the man who shows them game." He was active in the impeachment of Somers, Montague, the Duke of Portland, and the Earl of Oxford for their negotiation of the Partition Treaties. In later years he said he had acted here in ignorance, and justified those treaties.

James II. died at St. Germains, a pensioner of France, aged sixty-eight, on the 6th of September, 1701.

His pretensions to the English throne passed to the son, who had been born on the 10th of June, 1688, and whose birth had hastened on the Revolution. That son, James Francis Edward Stuart, who was only thirteen years old at his father's death, is known sometimes in history as the Old Pretender; the Young Pretender being his son Charles Edward, whose defeat at Culloden in 1746 destroyed the last faint hope of a restoration of the Stuarts. It is with the young heir to the pretensions of James II. that the story of the life of Bolingbroke becomes concerned.

King William III. died on the 8th of March, 1702, and was succeeded by James II.'s daughter Anne, who was then thirty-eight years old, and had been married when in her nineteenth year to Prince George of Denmark. She was a good wife and a good, simple-minded woman; a much-troubled mother, who had lost five children in their infancy, besides one who survived to be a boy of eleven and had died in the year 1700. As his death left the succession to the Crown unsettled, an Act of Settlement, passed on the 12th of June, 1701, had provided that, in case of failure of direct heirs to the throne, the Crown should pass to the next Protestant in succession, who was Sophia, wife of the Elector of Hanover. The Electress Sophia was daughter of the Princess Elizabeth who had married the Elector Palatine in 1613, granddaughter, therefore, of James I. She was more than seventy years old when Queen Anne began her reign. For ardent young Tories, who had no great interest in the limitation of authority or enthusiasm for a Protestant succession, it was no treason to think, though it would be treason to say, that the old Electress and her more than forty-year-old German son George, gross-minded and clumsy, did not altogether shut out hope for the succession of a more direct heir to the Crown.

In 1704 St. John was Secretary at War when Harley was Secretary of State, and he remained in office till 1708, when the Whigs came in under Marlborough and Godolphin, and St. John's successor was his rival Robert Walpole. St. John retired then for two year from public life to his country seat at Bucklersbury in Berkshire, which had come to him, through his wife, by the death of his wife's father the year before. He was thirty years old, the most brilliant of the rising statesmen; impatient of Harley as a leader and of Walpole as his younger rival from the other side, both of them men who, in his eyes, were dull and slow. St. John's quick intellect, though eager and impatient of successful rivalry, had its philosophic turn. During these two years of retirement he indulged the calmer love of study and thought, whose genius he said once, in a letter to Lord Bathurst "On the True use of Retirement and Study," "unlike the dream of Socrates, whispered so softly, that very often I heard him not, in the hurry of those passions by which I was transported. Some calmer hours there were; in them I hearkened to him. Reflection had often its turn, and the love of study and the desire of knowledge have never quite abandoned me."

In 1710 the Whigs were out and Harley in again, with St. John in his ministry as Secretary of State. "I am thinking," wrote Swift to Stella, "what a veneration we used to have for Sir William Temple because he might have been Secretary of State at fifty; and here is a young fellow hardly thirty in that employment."

It was the policy of the Tories to put an end to the war with France, that was against all their political interests. The Whigs wished to maintain it as a safeguard against reaction in favour of the Pretender. In the peace negotiations nobody was so active as Secretary St. John. On one occasion, without consulting his colleagues, he wrote to the Duke of Ormond, who commanded the English army in the Netherlands: "Her Majesty, my lord, has reason to believe that we shall come to an agreement on the great article of the union of the two monarchies as soon as a courier sent from Versailles to Madrid can return; it is, therefore, the Queen's positive command to your grace, that you avoid engaging in any siege or hazarding a battle till you have further orders from her Majesty. I am at the same time directed to let your grace know that the Queen would have you disguise the receipt of this order; and that her Majesty thinks you cannot want pretences for conducting yourself so as to answer her ends without owning that which might at present have an ill effect if publicly known." He added as a postscript: "I had almost forgot to tell your grace that communication is given of this order to the

Court of France." The peace was right, but the way of making it was mean in more ways than one, and the friction between Harley and St. John steadily increased. St. John used his majority in the House for the expulsion of his rival Walpole and Walpole's imprisonment in the Tower upon charges of corruption. In 1712, when Harley had obtained for himself the Earldom of Oxford, St. John wanted an earldom too; and the Earldom of Bolingbroke, in the elder branch of his family, had lately become extinct. His ill-will to Harley was embittered by the fact that only the lower rank of Viscount was conceded to him, and he was sent from the House of Commons, where his influence was great, at the age of thirty-four, as Viscount Bolingbroke and Baron St. John. His father's congratulation on the peerage glanced at the perils of Jacobitism: "Well, Harry, I said you would be hanged, but now I see you'll be beheaded."

The Treaty of Utrecht, that closed the War of the Spanish Succession, was signed on the 11th of April (new style), 1713. Queen Anne died on the 1st of August, 1714, when time was not ripe for the reaction that Bolingbroke had hoped to see. His Letter to Windham frankly leaves us to understand that in Queen Anne's reign the possible succession of James II.'s son, the Chevalier de St. George, had never been out of his mind.

The death of the Electress Sophia brought her son George to the throne. The Whigs triumphed, and Lord Bolingbroke was politically ruined. He was dismissed from office before the end of the month. On the 26th of March, 1715, he escaped to France, in disguise of a valet to the French messenger La Vigne. A Secret Committee of the House of Commons was, a few days afterwards, appointed to examine papers, and the result was Walpole's impeachment of Bolingbroke. He was, in September, 1715, in default of surrender, attainted of high treason, and his name was erased from the roll of peers. His own account of his policy will be found in this letter to his friend Sir William Windham, in which the only weak feature is the bitterness of Bolingbroke's resentment against Harley.

When he went in exile to France, Bolingbroke remained only a few days in Paris before retiring to St. Clair, near Vienne, in Dauphiny. His Letter to Windham tells how he became Secretary of State to the

Pretender, and how little influence he could obtain over the Jacobite counsels. The hopeless Rebellion of 1715, in Scotland, Bolingbroke laboured in vain to delay until there might be some chance of success. The death of Louis XIV., on the 1st of September in that year, had removed the last prop of a falling cause.

Some part of Bolingbroke's forfeited property was returned to his wife, who pleaded in vain for the reversal of his attainder. Bolingbroke was ill-used by the Pretender and abused by the Jacobites. He had been writing philosophical "Reflections upon Exile," but when he found himself thus attacked on both sides Bolingbroke resolved to cast Jacobitism to the winds, speak out like a man, and vindicate himself in a way that might possibly restore him to the service of his country. So in April, 1717, at the age of thirty-nine, he began work upon what is justly considered the best of his writings, his Letter to Sir William Windham.

Windham was a young Tory politician of good family and great wealth, who had married a daughter of the Duke of Somerset, and had been accepted by the Tories in the House of Commons as a leader, after Henry St. John had been sent to the House of Lords. Windham was "Dear Willie" to Bolingbroke, a constant friend, and in 1715 he was sent to the Tower as a Jacobite. But he had powerful connections, was kindly and not dangerous, and was soon back in his place in the House fighting the Whigs. The Letter to Windham was finished in the summer of 1717. Its frankness was only suited to the prospect of a pardon. It was found that there was no such prospect, and the Letter was not published until 1753, a year or two after its writer's death.

Bolingbroke's first wife died in November, 1718. He married in 1720 a Marquise de Villette, with whom he lived on an estate called La Source, near Orleans, at the source of the small river Loiret. There he talked and wrote philosophy. His pardon was obtained in May, 1723. In 1725 he was allowed by Act of Parliament the possession of his family inheritance; but as the attainder was not reversed he could never again sit in Parliament. So he came home in 1725, and bought an estate at Dawley, near Uxbridge. There he philosophised in his own way and played at farming, discoursed with Pope and plied his pen against the Whigs. In his letter to Pope, Bolingbroke writes of ministers of religion as if they had no other function than to maintain theological dogmas, and draws a false conclusion from false premisses. He died on the 12th of December, 1751.

H.M.

A LETTER TO SIR WILLIAM WINDHAM

I was well enough acquainted with the general character of mankind, and in particular with that of my own countrymen, to expect
to be as much out of the minds of the Tories during my exile as if
we had never lived and acted together. I depended on being forgot
by them, and was far from imagining it possible that I should be
remembered only to be condemned loudly by one half of them, and
to be tacitly censured by the greatest part of the other half. As soon
as I was separated from the Pretender and his interest, I declared
myself to be so; and I gave directions for writing into England what
I judged sufficient to put my friends on their guard against any
surprise concerning an event which it was their interest, as well as
mine, that they should be very rightly informed about.

As soon as the Pretender's adherents began to clamour against me
in this country, and to disperse their scandal by circular letters everywhere else, I gave directions for writing into England again. Their
groundless articles of accusation were refuted, and enough was said
to give my friends a general idea of what had happened to me, and
at least to make them suspend the fixing any opinion till such time
as I should be able to write more fully and plainly to them myself.
To condemn no person unheard is a rule of natural equity, which
we see rarely violated in Turkey, or in the country where I am writing: that it would not be so with me in Great Britain, I confess that I
flattered myself. I dwelt securely in this confidence, and gave very
little attention to any of those scurrilous methods which were taken
about this time to blast my reputation. The event of things has
shown that I trusted too much to my own innocence, and to the
justice of my old friends.

It was obvious that the Chevalier and the Earl of Mar hoped to load
me with the imputation of treachery, incapacity, or neglect: it was
indifferent to them of which. If they could ascribe to one of those
their not being supported from France, they imagined that they
should justify their precipitate flight from Scotland, which many of
their fastest friends exclaimed against; and that they should varnish

over that original capital fault, the drawing the Highlanders together in arms at the time and in the manner in which it was done.

The Scotch, who fell at once from all the sanguine expectations with
which they had been soothed, and who found themselves reduced
to despair, were easy to be incensed; they had received no support
whatever, and it was natural for them rather to believe that they
failed of this support by my fault, than to imagine their general had
prevailed on them to rise in the very point of time when it was impossible that they should be supported from France, or from any
other part of the world. The Duke of Ormond, who had been the
bubble of his own popularity, was enough out of humour with the
general turn of affairs to be easily set against any particular man.
The emissaries of this Court, whose commission was to amuse, had
imposed upon him all along; and there were other busy people who
thought to find their account in having him to themselves. I had
never been in his secret whilst we were in England together: and
from his first coming into France he was either prevailed upon by
others, or, which I rather believe, he concurred with others, to keep
me out of it. The perfect indifference I showed whether I was in it or
no, might carry him from acting separately, to act against me.

The whole tribe of Irish and other papists were ready to seize the
first opportunity of venting their spleen against a man, who had
constantly avoided all intimacy with them; who acted in the same
cause, but on a different principle, and who meant no one thing in
the world less than raising them to the advantages which they expected.

That these several persons, for the reasons I have mentioned, should
join in a cry against me, is not very marvellous; the contrary would
be so to a man who knows them as well as I do. But that the English
Tories should serve as echoes to them - nay more, that my character
should continue doubtful at best amongst you, when those who first
propagated the slander are become ashamed of railing without
proof, and have dropped the clamour, - this I own that I never expected; and I may be allowed to say, that as it is an extreme surprise, so it shall be a lesson to me.

The Whigs impeached and attainted me. They went farther - at least, in my way of thinking, that step was more cruel than all the others - by a partial representation of facts, and pieces of facts, put together as it best suited their purpose, and published to the whole world, they did all that in them lay to expose me for a fool, and to brand me for a knave. But then I had deserved this abundantly at their hands, according to the notions of party-justice. The Tories have not indeed impeached nor attainted me; but they have done, and are still doing something very like to that which I took worse of the Whigs than the impeachment and attainder: and this, after I have shown an inviolable attachment to the service, and almost an implicit obedience to the will of the party; when I am actually an outlaw, deprived of my honours, stripped of my fortune, and cut off from my family and my country, for their sakes.

Some of the persons who have seen me here, and with whom I have had the pleasure to talk of you, may, perhaps, have told you that, far from being oppressed by that storm of misfortunes in which I have been tossed of late, I bear up against it with firmness enough, and even with alacrity. It is true, I do so; but it is true likewise that the last burst of the cloud has gone near to overwhelm me. From our enemies we expect evil treatment of every sort, we are prepared for it, we are animated by it, and we sometimes triumph in it; but when our friends abandon us, when they wound us, and when they take, to do this, an occasion where we stand the most in need of their support, and have the best title to it, the firmest mind finds it hard to resist.

Nothing kept up my spirits when I was first reduced to the very circumstances I now describe so much as the consideration of the delusions under which I knew that the Tories lay, and the hopes I entertained of being able soon to open their eyes, and to justify my conduct. I expected that friendship, or, if that principle failed, curiosity at least, would move the party to send over some person from whose report they might have both sides of the question laid before them. Though this expectation be founded in reason, and you want to be informed at least as much as I do to be justified, yet I have hitherto flattered myself with it in vain. To repair this misfortune, therefore, as far as lies in my power, I resolve to put into writing the sum of what I should have said in that case. These papers shall lie by me till time and accidents produce some occasion of communicating them to you. The true occasion of doing it with advantage to the party will probably be lost; but they will remain a monument of my justification to posterity. At worst, if even this fails me, I am sure of one satisfaction in writing them: the satisfaction of unburdening my mind to a friend, and of stating before an equitable judge the account, as I apprehend it to stand, between the Tories and myself - "Quantum humano consilio efficere potui, circumspectis rebus meis omnibus, rationibusque subductis, summam feci cogitationum mearum omnium, quam tibi, si potero, breviter exponam."

It is necessary to my design that I call to your mind the state of affairs in Britain from the latter part of the year 1710 to the beginning of the year 1715, about which time we parted. I go no farther back because the part which I acted before that time, in the first essays I made in public affairs, was the part of a Tory, and so far of a piece with that which I acted afterwards. Besides, the things which preceded this space of time had no immediate influence on those which happened since that time, whereas the strange events which we have seen fall out in the king's reign were owing in a great measure to what was done, or neglected to be done, in the last four years of the queen's. The memory of these events being fresh, I shall dwell as little as possible upon them; it will be sufficient that I make a rough sketch of the face of the Court, and of the conduct of the several parties during that time. Your memory will soon furnish the colours which I shall omit to lay, and finish up the picture.

From the time at which I left Britain I had not the advantage of acting under the eyes of the party which I served, nor of being able from time to time to appeal to their judgment. The gross of what happened has appeared; but the particular steps which led to those events have been either concealed or misrepresented - concealed from the nature of them or misrepresented by those with whom I never agreed perfectly except in thinking that they and I were extremely unfit to continue embarked in the same bottom together. It will, therefore, be proper to descend under this head to a more particular relation.

In the summer of the year 1710 the Queen was prevailed upon to change her Parliament and her Ministry. The intrigue of the Earl of Oxford might facilitate the means, the violent prosecution of Sacheverel, and other unpopular measures, might create the occasion and encourage her in the resolution; but the true original cause was the personal ill-usage which she received in her private life and in some trifling instances of the exercise of her power, for indulgence in which she would certainly have left the reins of government in those hands which had held them ever since her accession to the throne.

I am afraid that we came to Court in the same dispositions as all parties have done; that the principal spring of our actions was to have the government of the state in our hands; that our principal views were the conservation of this power, great employments to ourselves, and great opportunities of rewarding those who had helped to raise us, and of hurting those who stood in opposition to us. It is, however, true that with these considerations of private and party interest there were others intermingled which had for their object the public good of the nation - at least what we took to be such.

We looked on the political principles which had generally prevailed in our government from the Revolution in 1688 to be destructive of our true interest, to have mingled us too much in the affairs of the Continent, to tend to the impoverishing our people, and to the loosening the bands of our constitution in Church and State. We supposed the Tory party to be the bulk of the landed interest, and to have no contrary influence blended into its composition. We supposed the Whigs to be the remains of a party formed against the ill designs of the Court under King Charles II., nursed up into strength and applied to contrary uses by King William III., and yet still so weak as to lean for support on the Presbyterians and the other sectaries, on the Bank and the other corporations, on the Dutch and the other Allies. From hence we judged it to follow that they had been forced, and must continue so, to render the national interest subservient to the interest of those who lent them an additional strength, without which they could never be the prevalent party. The view, therefore, of those amongst us who thought in this manner was to

improve the Queen's favour, to break the body of the Whigs, to
render their supports useless to them, and to fill the employments
of the kingdom, down to the meanest, with Tories. We imagined
that such measures, joined to the advantages of our numbers and
our property, would secure us against all attempts during her reign,
and that we should soon become too considerable not to make our
terms in all events which might happen afterwards: concerning
which, to speak truly, I believe few or none of us had any very settled resolution.

In order to bring these purposes about, I verily think that the persecution of Dissenters entered into no man's head. By the Bills for
preventing Occasional Conformity and the growth of schism, it was
hoped that their sting would be taken away. These Bills were
thought necessary for our party interest, and, besides, were deemed
neither unreasonable nor unjust. The good of society may require
that no person should be deprived of the protection of the Government on account of his opinions in religious matters; but it does not
follow from hence that men ought to be trusted in any degree with
the preservation of the Establishment, who must, to be consistent
with their principles, endeavour the subversion of what is established. An indulgence to consciences, which the prejudice of education and long habits have rendered scrupulous, may be agreeable to
the rules of good policy and of humanity, yet will it hardly follow
from hence that a government is under any obligation to indulge a
tenderness of conscience to come, or to connive at the propagating
of these prejudices and at the forming of these habits. The evil effect
is without remedy, and may, therefore, deserve indulgence; but the
evil cause is to be prevented, and can, therefore, be entitled to none.
Besides this, the Bills I am speaking of, rather than to enact anything
new, seemed only to enforce the observation of ancient laws which
had been judged necessary for the security of the Church and State
at a time when the memory of the ruin of both, and of the hands by
which that ruin had been wrought, was fresh in the minds of men.

The Bank, the East India Company, and in general the moneyed
interest, had certainly nothing to apprehend like what they feared,
or affected to fear, from the Tories - an entire subversion of their
property. Multitudes of our own party would have been wounded

by such a blow. The intention of those who were the warmest
seemed to me to go no farther than restraining their influence on the
Legislature, and on matters of State; and finding at a proper season
means to make them contribute to the support and ease of a government under which they enjoyed advantages so much greater
than the rest of their fellow-subjects. The mischievous consequence
which had been foreseen and foretold too, at the establishment of
those corporations, appeared visibly. The country gentlemen were
vexed, put to great expenses and even baffled by them in their elections; and among the members of every parliament numbers were
immediately or indirectly under their influence. The Bank had been
extravagant enough to pull off the mask; and, when the Queen
seemed to intend a change in her ministry, they had deputed some
of their members to represent against it. But that which touched
sensibly even those who were but little affected by other considerations, was the prodigious inequality between the condition of the
moneyed men and of the rest of the nation. The proprietor of the
land, and the merchant who brought riches home by the returns of
foreign trade, had during two wars borne the whole immense load
of the national expenses; whilst the lender of money, who added
nothing to the common stock, throve by the public calamity, and
contributed not a mite to the public charge.

As to the Allies, I saw no difference of opinion among all those who
came to the head of affairs at this time. Such of the Tories as were in
the system above mentioned, such of them as deserted soon after
from us, and such of the Whigs as had upon this occasion deserted
to us, seemed equally convinced of the unreasonableness, and even
of the impossibility, of continuing the war on the same dispropor-
tionate footing. Their universal sense was, that we had taken, except
the part of the States General, the whole burden of the war upon us,
and even a proportion of this; while the entire advantage was to
accrue to others: that this had appeared very grossly in 1709, and
1710, when preliminaries were insisted upon, which contained all
that the Allies, giving the greatest loose to their wishes, could desire, and little or nothing on the behalf of Great Britain: that the war,
which had been begun for the security of the Allies, was continued
for their grandeur: that the ends proposed, when we engaged in it,
might have been answered long before, and therefore that the first

favourable occasion ought to be seized of making peace; which we thought to be the interest of our country, and which appeared to all mankind, as well as to us, to be that of our party.

These were in general the views of the Tories: and for the part I acted in the prosecution of them, as well as of all the measures accessory to them, I may appeal to mankind. To those who had the opportunity of looking behind the curtain I may likewise appeal, for the difficulties which lay in my way, and for the particular discouragements which I met with. A principal load of parliamentary and foreign affairs in their ordinary course lay upon me: the whole negotiation of the peace, and of the troublesome invidious steps preliminary to it, as far as they could be transacted at home, were thrown upon me. I continued in the House of Commons during that important session which preceded the peace; and which, by the spirit shown through the whole course of it, and by the resolutions taken in it, rendered the conclusion of the treaties practicable. After this I was dragged into the House of Lords in such a manner as to make my promotion a punishment, not a reward; and was there left to defend the treaties almost alone.

It would not have been hard to have forced the Earl of Oxford to use me better. His good intentions began to be very much doubted of; the truth is, no opinion of his sincerity had ever taken root in the party, and, which was worse perhaps for a man in his station, the opinion of his capacity began to fall apace. He was so hard pushed in the House of Lords in the beginning of 1712 that he had been forced, in the middle of the session, to persuade the Queen to make a promotion of twelve peers at once, which was an unprecedented and invidious measure, to be excused by nothing but the necessity, and hardly by that. In the House of Commons his credit was low and my reputation very high. You know the nature of that assembly; they grow, like hounds, fond of the man who shows them game, and by whose halloo they are used to be encouraged. The thread of the negotiations, which could not stand still a moment without going back, was in my hands, and before another man could have made himself master of the business much time would have been lost, and great inconveniences would have followed. Some, who opposed the Court soon after, began to waver then, and if I had not wanted the inclination I should have wanted no help to do mischief. I knew the way of quitting my employments and of retiring from Court when the service of my party required it; but I could not bring myself up to that resolution, when the consequence of it must have been the breaking my party and the distress of the public affairs. I thought my mistress treated me ill, but the sense of that duty which I owed her came in aid of other considerations, and prevailed over my resentment. These sentiments, indeed, are so much out of fashion that a man who avows them is in danger of passing for a bubble in the world; yet they were, in the conjuncture I speak of, the true motives of my conduct, and you saw me go on as cheerfully in the troublesome and dangerous work assigned me as if I had been under the utmost satisfaction. I began, indeed, in my heart to renounce the friendship which till that time I had preserved inviolable for Oxford. I was not aware of all his treachery, nor of the base and little means which he employed then, and continued to employ afterwards, to ruin me in the opinion of the Queen and everywhere else. I saw, however, that he had no friendship for any-body, and that with respect to me, instead of having the ability to render that merit, which I endeavoured to acquire, an addition of strength to himself, it became the object of his jealousy and a reason for undermining me. In this temper of mind I went on till the great work of the peace was consummated and the treaty signed at Utrecht; after which a new and more melancholy scene for the par-ty, as well as for me, opened itself.

I am far from thinking the treaties, or the negotiations which led to them, exempt from faults. Many were made no doubt in both by those who were concerned in them; by myself in the first place, and many were owing purely to the opposition they met with in every step of their progress. I never look back on this great event, passed as it is, without a secret emotion of mind; when I compare the vast-ness of the undertaking and the importance of its success, with the means employed to bring it about, and with those which were em-ployed to traverse it. To adjust the pretensions and to settle the interests of so many princes and states as were engaged in the late war would appear, when considered simply and without any ad-ventitious difficulty, a work of prodigious extent. But this was not all. Each of our Allies thought himself entitled to raise his demands

to the most extravagant height. They had been encouraged to this,
first, by the engagements which we had entered into with several of
them, with some to draw them into the war, with others to prevail
on them to continue it; and, secondly, by the manner in which we
had treated with France in 1709 and 1710. Those who intended to tie
the knot of the war as hard, and to render the coming at a peace as
impracticable as they could, had found no method so effectual as
that of leaving everyone at liberty to insist on all he could think of,
and leaving themselves at liberty, even if these concessions should
be made, to break the treaty by ulterior demands. That this was the
secret I can make no doubt after the confession of one of the pleni-
potentiaries who transacted these matters, and who communicated
to me and to two others of the Queen's Ministers an instance of the
Duke of Marlborough's management at a critical moment, when the
French Ministers at Gertrudenberg seemed inclinable to come into
an expedient for explaining the thirty-seventh article of the preliminaries, which could not have been refused. Certain it is that the
King of France was at that time in earnest to execute the article of
Philip's abdication, and therefore the expedients for adjusting what
related to this article would easily enough have been found, if on
our part there had been a real intention of concluding. But there was
no such intention, and the plan of those who meant to prolong the
war was established among the Allies as the plan which ought to be
followed whenever a peace came to be treated. The Allies imagined
that they had a right to obtain at least everything which had been
demanded for them respectively, and it was visible that nothing less
would content them. These considerations set the vastness of the
undertaking in a sufficient light.

The importance of succeeding in the work of the peace was equally
great to Europe, to our country, to our party, to our persons, to the
present age, and to future generations. But I need not take pains to
prove what no man will deny. The means employed to bring it
about were in no degree proportionable. A few men, some of whom
had never been concerned in business of this kind before, and most
of whom put their hands for a long time to it faintly and timorously,
were the instruments of it. The Minister who was at their head
showed himself every day incapable of that attention, that method,
that comprehension of different matters, which the first post in such

a Government as ours requires in quiet times. He was the first spring of all our motion by his credit with the Queen, and his concurrence was necessary to everything we did by his rank in the State, and yet this man seemed to be sometimes asleep and sometimes at play. He neglected the thread of business, which was carried on for this reason with less dispatch and less advantage in the proper channels, and he kept none in his own hands. He negotiated, indeed, by fits and starts, by little tools and indirect ways, and thus his activity became as hurtful as his indolence, of which I could produce some remarkable instances. No good effect could flow from such a conduct. In a word, when this great affair was once engaged, the zeal of particular men in their several provinces drove it forward, though they were not backed by the concurrent force of the whole Administration, nor had the common helps of advice till it was too late, till the very end of the negotiations; even in matters, such as that of commerce, which they could not be supposed to understand. That this is a true account of the means used to arrive at the peace, and a true character of that Administration in general, I believe the whole Cabinet Council of that time will bear me witness. Sure I am that most of them have joined with me in lamenting this state of things whilst it subsisted, and all those who were employed as Ministers in the several parts of the treaty felt sufficiently the difficulties which this strange management often reduced them to. I am confident they have not forgotten them.

If the means employed to bring the peace about were feeble, and in one respect contemptible, those employed to break the negotiation were strong and formidable. As soon as the first suspicion of a treaty's being on foot crept abroad in the world the whole alliance united with a powerful party in the nation to obstruct it. From that hour to the moment the Congress of Utrecht finished, no one measure possible to be taken was omitted to traverse every advance that was made in this work, to intimidate, to allure, to embarrass every person concerned in it. This was done without any regard either to decency or good policy, and from hence it soon followed that passion and humour mingled themselves on each side. A great part of what we did for the peace, and of what others did against it, can be accounted for on no other principle. The Allies were broken among themselves before they began to treat with the common enemy. The matter did not mend in the course of the treaty, and France and Spain, but especially the former, profited of this disunion.

Whoever makes the comparison, which I have touched upon, will see the true reasons which rendered the peace less answerable to the success of the war than it might and than it ought to have been. Judgment has been passed in this case as the different passions or interests of men have inspired them. But the real cause lay in the constitution of our Ministry, and much more in the obstinate opposition which we met with from the Whigs and from the Allies. However, sure it is that the defects of the peace did not occasion the desertions from the Tory party which happened about this time, nor those disorders in the Court which immediately followed.

Long before the purport of the treaties could be known, those Whigs who had set out with us in 1710 began to relapse back to their party. They had among us shared the harvest of a new Ministry, and, like prudent persons, they took measures in time to have their share in that of a new Government.

The whimsical or the Hanover Tories continued zealous in appearance with us till the peace was signed. I saw no people so eager for the conclusion of it. Some of them were in such haste that they thought any peace preferable to the least delay, and omitted no instances to quicken their friends who were actors in it. As soon as the treaties were perfected and laid before the Parliament, the scheme of these gentlemen began to disclose itself entirely. Their love of the peace, like other passions, cooled by enjoyment. They grew nice about the construction of the articles, could come up to no direct approbation, and, being let into the secret of what was to happen, would not preclude themselves from the glorious advantage of rising on the ruins of their friends and of their party.

The danger of the succession and the badness of the peace were the two principles on which we were attacked. On the first the whimsical Tories joined the Whigs, and declared directly against their party. Although nothing is more certain than this truth: that there was at that time no formed design in the party, whatever views some particular men might have, against his Majesty's accession to the throne. On the latter, and most other points, they affected a most glorious neutrality.

Instead of gathering strength, either as a Ministry or as a party, we grew weaker every day. The peace had been judged, with reason, to be the only solid foundation whereupon we could erect a Tory system; and yet when it was made we found ourselves at a full stand. Nay, the very work which ought to have been the basis of our strength was in part demolished before our eyes, and we were stoned with the ruins of it. Whilst this was doing, Oxford looked on as if he had not been a party to all which had passed; broke now and then a jest, which savoured of the Inns of Court and the bad company in which he had been bred. And on those occasions where his station obliged him to speak of business, was absolutely unintelligible.

Whether this man ever had any determined view besides that of raising his family is, I believe, a problematical question in the world. My opinion is that he never had any other. The conduct of a Minister who proposes to himself a great and noble object, and who pursues it steadily, may seem for a while a riddle to the world; especially in a Government like ours, where numbers of men, different in their characters and different in their interests, are at all times to be managed; where public affairs are exposed to more accidents and greater hazards than in other countries; and where, by consequence, he who is at the head of business will find himself often distracted by measures which have no relation to his purpose, and obliged to bend himself to things which are in some degree contrary to his main design. The ocean which environs us is an emblem of our government, and the pilot and the Minister are in similar circumstances. It seldom happens that either of them can steer a direct course, and they both arrive at their port by means which frequently seem to carry them from it. But as the work advances the conduct of him who leads it on with real abilities clears up, the appearing inconsistencies are reconciled, and when it is once consummated the whole shows itself so uniform, so plain, and so natural, that every dabbler in politics will be apt to think he could have done the same. But, on the other hand, a man who proposes no such object, who substitutes artifice in the place of ability, who, instead of leading

parties and governing accidents, is eternally agitated backwards
and forwards by both, who begins every day something new, and
carries nothing on to perfection, may impose awhile on the world;
but a little sooner or a little later the mystery will be revealed, and
nothing will be found to be couched under it but a thread of pitiful
expedients, the ultimate end of which never extended farther than
living from day to day. Which of these pictures resembles Oxford
most you will determine. I am sorry to be obliged to name him so
often, but how is it possible to do otherwise while I am speaking of
times wherein the whole turn of affairs depended on his motions
and character?

I have heard, and I believe truly, that when he returned to Windsor
in the autumn of 1713, after the marriage of his son, he pressed extremely to have him created Duke of Newcastle or Earl of Clare, and
the Queen presuming to hesitate on so extraordinary a proposal, he
resented this hesitation in a manner which little became a man who
had been so lately raised by the profusion of her favours upon him.
Certain it is, that he began then to show a still greater remissness in
all parts of his Ministry, and to affect to say that from such a time,
the very time I am speaking of, he took no share in the direction of
affairs, or words to that effect.

He pretended to have discovered intrigues which were set on foot
against him, and particularly he complained of the advantage which
was taken of his absence during the journey he made at his son's
marriage to undermine him with the Queen. He is naturally inclined to believe the worst, which I take to be a certain mark of a
mean spirit and a wicked soul. At least, I am sure that the contrary
quality, when it is not due to weakness of understanding, is the fruit
of a generous temper and an honest heart. Prone to judge ill of all
mankind, he will rarely be seduced by his credulity, but I never
knew a man so capable of being the bubble of his distrust and jealousy. He was so in this case, although the Queen, who could not be
ignorant of the truth, said enough to undeceive him. But to be undeceived, and to own himself so, was not his play. He hoped by
cunning to varnish over his want of faith and of ability. He was
desirous to make the world impute the extraordinary part, or, to
speak more properly, the no part, which he acted with the staff of

Treasurer in his hand, to the Queen's withdrawing her favour from
him and to his friends abandoning him - pretences utterly groundless when he first made them, and which he brought to be real at
last. Even the winter before the Queen's death, when his credit began to wane apace, he might have regained it; he might have reconciled himself perfectly with all his ancient friends, and have acquired the confidence of the whole party. I say he might have done
all this, because I am persuaded that none of those I have named
were so convinced of his perfidy, so jaded with his yoke, or so much
piqued personally against him as I was; and yet if he would have
exerted himself in concert with us to improve the few advantages
which were left us and to ward off the visible danger which threatened our persons and our party, I would have stifled my private
animosity and would have acted under him with as much zeal as
ever. But he was incapable of taking such a turn. The sum of all his
policy had been to amuse the Whigs, the Tories, and the Jacobites as
long as he could, and to keep his power as long as he amused them.
When it became impossible to amuse mankind any longer, he appeared plainly at the end of his line.

By a secret correspondence with the late Earl of Halifax, and by the
intrigues of his brother and other fanatical relations, he had endeavoured to keep some hold on the Whigs.

The Tories were attached to him at first by the heat of a revolution
in the Ministry, by their hatred of the people who were discarded,
and by the fond hopes which it is easy to give at the setting out of a
new administration. Afterwards he held out the peace in prospect to
them and to the Jacobites separately, as an event which must be
brought about before he could effectually serve either. You cannot
have forgot how things which we pressed were put off upon every
occasion till the peace; the peace was to be the date of a new administration, and the period at which the millenary year of Toryism
should begin. Thus were the Tories at that time amused; and since
my exile I have had the opportunity of knowing certainly and circumstantially that the Jacobites were treated in the same manner,
and that the Pretender was made, through the French Minister, to
expect that measures should be taken for his restoration as soon as
the peace had rendered them practicable. He was to attempt noth-

ing, his partisans were to lie still, Oxford undertook for all.

After many delays, fatal to the general interest of Europe, this peace was signed: and the only considerable thing which he brought about afterwards was the marriage I have mentioned above; and by it an accession of riches and honour to a family whose estate was very mean, and whose illustration before this time I never met with anywhere, but in the vain discourses which he used to hold over claret. If he kept his word with any of the parties above-mentioned, it must be supposed that he did so with the Whigs; for as to us, we saw nothing after the peace but increase of mortification and nearer approaches to ruin. Not a step was made towards completing the settlement of Europe, which the treaties of Utrecht and Radstadt left imperfect; towards fortifying and establishing the Tory party; towards securing those who had been the principal actors in this administration against future events. We had proceeded in a confidence that these things should immediately follow the conclusion of the peace: he had never, I dare swear, entertained a thought concerning them. As soon as the last hand was given to the fortune of his family, he abandoned his mistress, his friends, and his party, who had borne him so many years on their shoulders: and I was present when this want of faith was reproached him in the plainest and strongest terms by one of the honestest men in Britain, and before some of the most considerable Tories. Even his impudence failed him on this occasion: he did not so much as attempt an excuse.

He could not keep his word which he had given the Pretender and his adherents, because he had formed no party to support him in such a design. He was sure of having the Whigs against him if he made the attempt, and he was not sure of having the Tories for him.

In this state of confusion and distress, to which he had reduced himself and us, you remember the part he acted. He was the spy of the Whigs, and voted with us in the morning against those very questions which he had penned the night before with Walpole and others. He kept his post on terms which no man but he would have held it on, neither submitting to the Queen, nor complying with his friends. He would not, or he could not, act with us; and he resolved

that we should not act without him as long as he could hinder it.
The Queen's health was very precarious, and at her death he hoped
by these means to deliver us up, bound as it were hand and foot, to
our adversaries. On the foundation of this merit he flattered himself
that he had gained some of the Whigs, and softened at least the rest
of the party to him. By his secret negotiations at Hanover, he took it
for granted that he was not only reconciled to that Court, but that he
should, under his present Majesty's reign, have as much credit as he
had enjoyed under that of the Queen. He was weak enough to boast
of this, and to promise his good offices voluntarily to several: for no
man was weak enough to think them worth being solicited. In a
word, you must have heard that he answered to Lord Dartmouth
and to Mr. Bromley, that one should keep the Privy Seal, and the
other the seals of Secretary; and that Lord Cowper makes no scruple
of telling how he came to offer him the seals of Chancellor. When
the King arrived, he went to Greenwich with an affectation of pomp
and of favour. Against his suspicious character, he was once in his
life the bubble of his credulity; and this delusion betrayed him into
a punishment more severe in my sense than all which has happened
to him since, or than perpetual exile; he was affronted in the manner
in which he was presented to the King. The meanest subject would
have been received with goodness, the most obnoxious with an air
of indifference; but he was received with the most distinguishing
contempt. This treatment he had in the face of the nation. The King
began his reign, in this instance, with punishing the ingratitude, the
perfidy, the insolence, which had been shown to his predecessor.
Oxford fled from Court covered with shame, the object of the deri-
sion of the Whigs and of the indignation of the Tories.

The Queen might, if she had pleased, have saved herself from all
those mortifications she met with during the last months of her
reign, and her servants and the Tory party from those misfortunes
which they endured during the same time; perhaps from those
which they have fallen into since her death. When she found that
the peace, from the conclusion of which she expected ease and quiet, brought still greater trouble upon her; when she saw the weakness of her Government, and the confusion of her affairs increase
every day; when she saw her First Minister bewildered and unable
to extricate himself or her; in fine, when the negligence of his public

conduct, and the sauciness of his private behaviour had rendered him insupportable to her, and she took the resolution of laying him aside, there was a strength still remaining sufficient to have supported her Government, to have fulfilled in great part the expectations of the Tories, and to have constituted both them and the Ministers in such a situation as would have left them little to apprehend. Some designs were, indeed, on foot which might have produced very great disorders: Oxford's conduct had given much occasion to them, and with the terror of them he endeavoured to intimidate the Queen. But expedients were not hard to be found by which those designs might have been nipped in the bud, or else by which the persons who promoted them might have been induced to lay them aside. But that fatal irresolution inherent to the Stuart race hung upon her. She felt too much inward resentment to be able to conceal his disgrace from him; yet, after he had made this discovery, she continued to trust all her power in his hands.

No people ever were in such a condition as ours continued to be from the autumn of 1713 to the summer following. The Queen's health sank every day. The attack which she had in the winter at Windsor served as a warning both to those who wished, and to those who feared her death, to expect it. The party which opposed the court had been continually gaining strength by the weakness of our administration: and at this time their numbers were vastly increased, and their spirit was raised by the near prospect of the succession taking place. We were not at liberty to exert the strength we had. We saw our danger, and many of us saw the true means of avoiding it; but whilst the magic wand was in the same hands, this knowledge served only to increase our uneasiness; and, whether we would or no, we were forced with our eyes open to walk on towards the precipice. Every moment we became less able, if the Queen lived, to support her Government; if she died, to secure ourselves. One side was united in a common view, and acted upon a uniform plan: the other had really none at all. We knew that we were out of favour at the Court of Hanover, that we were represented there as Jacobites, and that the Elector, his present Majesty, had been rendered publicly a party to that opposition, in spite of which we made the peace: and yet we neither had taken, nor could take in our present circumstances, any measures to be better or worse there.

Thus we languished till the 27th of July, 1714, when the Queen dismissed the Treasurer. On the Friday following, she fell into an apoplexy, and died on Sunday the 1st of August.

You do me, I daresay, the justice to believe that whilst this state of things lasted I saw very well, how little mention soever I might make of it at the time, that no man in the Ministry, or in the party, was so much exposed as myself. I could expect no quarter from the Whigs, for I had deserved none. There were persons amongst them for whom I had great esteem and friendship; yet neither with these, nor with any others, had I preserved a secret correspondence, which might be of use to me in the day of distress: and besides the general character of my party, I knew that particular prejudices were entertained against me at Hanover. The Whigs wanted nothing but an opportunity of attacking the peace, and it could hardly be imagined that they would stop there. In which case I knew that they could have hold on no man so much as myself: the instructions, the orders, the memorials had been drawn by me; the correspondence relating to it in France, and everywhere else, had been carried on by me; in a word, my hand appeared to almost every paper which had been writ in the whole course of the negotiation. To all these considerations I added that of the weight of personal resentment, which I had created against myself at home and abroad: in part unavoidably, by the share I was obliged to take in these affairs; and in part, if you will, unnecessarily, by the warmth of my temper, and by some unguarded expressions, for which I have no excuse to make but that which Tacitus makes for his father-in-law, Julius Agricola: "honestius putabam offendere, quam odisse."

Having this prospect of being distinguished from the rest of my party, in the common calamity, by severer treatment, I might have justified myself, by reason and by great authorities too, if I had made early provision, at least to be safe when I should be no longer useful. How I could have secured this point I do not think fit to explain: but certain it is that I made no one step towards it. I resolved not to abandon my party by turning Whig, or, which is worse a great deal, whimsical; nor to treat separately from it. I resolved to keep myself at liberty to act on a Tory bottom. If the Queen disgraced Oxford and continued to live afterwards, I knew we should have time and means to provide for our future safety: if the Queen died, and left us in the same unfortunate circumstances, I expected to suffer for and with the Tories; and I was prepared for it.

The thunder had long grumbled in the air; and yet when the bolt fell, most of our party appeared as much surprised as if they had had no reason to expect it. There was a perfect calm and universal submission through the whole kingdom. The Chevalier, indeed, set out as if his design had been to gain the coast and to embark for Great Britain; and the Court of France made a merit to themselves of stopping him and obliging him to return. But this, to my certain knowledge, was a farce acted by concert, to keep up an opinion of his character, when all opinion of his cause seemed to be at an end. He owned this concert to me at Bar, on the occasion of my telling him that he would have found no party ready to receive him, and that the enterprise would have been to the last degree extravagant. He was at this time far from having any encouragement: no party numerous enough to make the least disturbance was formed in his favour. On the King's arrival the storm arose. The menaces of the Whigs, backed by some very rash declarations, by little circumstances of humour which frequently offend more than real injuries, and by the entire change of all the persons in employment, blew up the coals.

At first many of the Tories had been made to entertain some faint hopes that they would be permitted to live in quiet. I have been assured that the King left Hanover in that resolution. Happy had it been for him and for us if he had continued in it; if the moderation of his temper had not been overborne by the violence of party, and his and the national interest sacrificed to the passions of a few. Others there were among the Tories who had flattered themselves with much greater expectations than these, and who had depended, not on such imaginary favour and dangerous advancement as was offered them afterwards, but on real credit and substantial power under the new government. Such impressions on the minds of men had rendered the two Houses of Parliament, which were then sitting, as good courtiers to King George as ever they had been to Queen Anne. But all these hopes being at once and with violence extinguished, despair succeeded in their room.

Our party began soon to act like men delivered over to their passions, and unguided by any other principle; not like men fired by a just resentment and a reasonable ambition to a bold undertaking. They treated the Government like men who were resolved not to live under it: and yet they took no one measure to support themselves against it. They expressed, without reserve or circumspection, an eagerness to join in any attempt against the Establishment which they had received and confirmed, and which many of them had courted but a few weeks before; and yet in the midst of all this bravery, when the election of the new Parliament came on, some of these very men acted with the coolness of those who are much better disposed to compound than to take arms.

The body of the Tories being in this temper, it is not to be wondered at if they heated one another, and began apace to turn their eyes towards the Pretender; and if those few who had already engaged with him, applied themselves to improve the conjuncture, and endeavoured to list a party for him.

I went, about a month after the Queen's death, as soon as the Seals were taken from me, into the country; and whilst I continued there, I felt the general disposition to Jacobitism increase daily among people of all ranks; amongst several who had been constantly distinguished by their aversion to that cause. But at my return to London in the month of February or March, 1715, a few weeks before I left England, I began for the first time in my whole life to perceive these general dispositions ripen into resolutions, and to observe some regular workings among many of our principal friends, which denoted a scheme of this kind. These workings, indeed, were very faint; for the persons concerned in carrying them on did not think it safe to speak too plainly to men who were, in truth, ill disposed to the Government because they neither found their account at present under it nor had been managed with art enough to leave them hopes of finding it hereafter, but who at the same time had not the least affection for the Pretender's person, nor any principle favourable to his interest.

This was the state of things when the new Parliament which his

Majesty had called assembled. A great majority of the elections had gone in favour of the Whigs; to which the want of concert among the Tories had contributed as much as the vigour of that party and the influence of the new Government. The Whigs came to the opening of this Parliament full of as much violence as could possess men who expected to make their court, to confirm themselves in power, and to gratify their resentments by the same measures. I have heard that it was a dispute among the Ministers how far this spirit should be indulged; and that the King was determined, or confirmed in a determination, to consent to the prosecutions, and to give the reins to the party, by the representations that were made to him that great difficulties would arise in the conduct of the Session if the Court should appear inclined to check this spirit, and by Mr. W - 's undertaking to carry all the business successfully through the House of Commons if they were at liberty. Such has often been the unhappy fate of our Princes: a real necessity sometimes, and sometimes a seeming one, has forced them to compound with a part of the nation at the expense of the whole; and the success of their business for one year has been purchased at the price of public disorder for many.

The conjuncture I am speaking of affords a memorable instance of this truth. If milder measures had been pursued, certain it is that the Tories had never universally embraced Jacobitism. The violence of the Whigs forced them into the arms of the Pretender. The Court and the party seemed to vie with one another which should go the greatest lengths in severity: and the Ministers, whose true interest it must at all times be to calm the minds of men, and who ought never to set the examples of extraordinary inquiries or extraordinary accusations, were upon this occasion the tribunes of the people.

The Council of Regency which began to sit as soon as the Queen died, acted like a council of the Holy Office. Whoever looked on the face of the nation saw everything quiet; not one of those symptoms appearing which must have shown themselves more or less at that moment if in reality there had been any measures taken during the former reign to defeat the Protestant succession. His Majesty ascended the throne with as little contradiction and as little trouble as ever a son succeeded a father in the possession of a private patrimony. But he who had the opportunity, which I had till my dismission, of seeing a great part of what passed in that Council, would have thought that there had been an opposition actually formed, that the new Establishment was attacked openly from without and betrayed from within.

The same disposition continued after the King's arrival. This political Inquisition went on with all the eagerness imaginable in seizing of papers, in ransacking the Queen's closet, and examining even her private letters. The Whigs had clamoured loudly, and affirmed in the face of the world that the nation had been sold to France, to Spain, to the Pretender; and whilst they endeavoured in vain, by very singular methods, to find some colour to justify what they had advanced without proof, they put themselves under an absolute necessity of grounding the most solemn prosecution on things whereof they might indeed have proof, but which would never pass for crimes before any judges but such as were parties at the same time.

In the King's first Speech from the Throne all the inflaming hints were given, and all the methods of violence were chalked out to the two Houses. The first steps in both were perfectly answerable; and, to the shame of the peerage be it spoken, I saw at that time several lords concur to condemn in one general vote all that they had approved of in a former Parliament by many particular resolutions. Among several bloody resolutions proposed and agitated at this time, the resolution of impeaching me of high treason was taken; and I took that of leaving England, not in a panic terror improved by the artifices of the Duke of Marlborough (whom I knew even at that time too well to act by his advice or information in any case), but on such grounds as the proceedings which soon followed sufficiently justified, and as I have never repented building upon. Those who blamed it in the first heat were soon after obliged to change their language; for what other resolution could I take? The method of prosecution designed against me would have put me immediately out of condition to act for myself, or to serve those who were less exposed than me, but who were, however, in danger. On the other hand, how few were there on whose assistance I could depend, or to whom I would, even in those circumstances, be obliged? The fer-

ment in the nation was wrought up to a considerable height; but
there was at that time no reason to expect that it could influence the
proceedings in Parliament in favour of those who should be ac-
cused. Left to its own movement, it was much more proper to
quicken than slacken the prosecutions; and who was there to guide
its motions? The Tories who had been true to one another to the last
were a handful, and no great vigour could be expected from them.
The Whimsicals, disappointed of the figure which they hoped to
make, began, indeed, to join their old friends. One of the principal
amongst them was so very good as to confess to me that if the Court
had called the servants of the late Queen to account, and had
stopped there, he must have considered himself as a judge, and
have acted according to his conscience on what should have appeared to him; but that war had been declared to the whole Tory
party, and that now the state of things was altered. This discourse
needed no commentary, and proved to me that I had never erred in
the judgment I made of this set of men. Could I then resolve to be
obliged to them, or to suffer with Oxford? As much as I still was
heated by the disputes in which I had been all my life engaged
against the Whigs, I would sooner have chose to owe my security to
their indulgence than to the assistance of the Whimsicals; but I
thought banishment, with all her train of evils, preferable to either. I
abhorred Oxford to that degree that I could not bear to be joined
with him in any case. Nothing, perhaps, contributed so much to
determine me as this sentiment. A sense of honour would not have
permitted me to distinguish between his case and mine own; and it
was worse than death to lie under the necessity of making them the
same, and of taking measures in concert with him.

I am now come to the time at which I left England, and have finished the first part of that deduction of facts which I proposed to lay
before you. I am hopeful that you will not think it altogether tedious
or unnecessary; for although very little of what I have said can be
new to you, yet this summary account will enable you with greater
ease to recall to your memory the passages of those four years
wherewith all that I am going to relate to you has an immediate and
necessary connection.

In what has been said I am far from making my own panegyric. I had not in those days so much merit as was ascribed to me, nor since that time have I had so little as the same persons allowed me. I committed, without dispute, many faults, and a greater man than I can pretend to be, constituted in the same circumstances, would not have kept clear of all; but with respect to the Tories I committed none. I carried the point of party honour to the height, and specified everything to my attachment to them during this period of time. Let us now examine whether I have done so during the rest.

When I arrived in France, about the end of March, 1715, the affairs of England were represented to me in another light than I had seen them in when I looked upon them with my own eyes very few weeks before. I found the persons who were detached to speak with me prepared to think that I came over to negotiate for the Pretender; and when they perceived that I was more ignorant than they imagined, I was assured by them that there would be suddenly a universal rising in England and Scotland. The leaders were named to me, their engagements specified, and many gentlemen, yourself among others, were reckoned upon for particular services, though I was certain you had never been treated with; from whence I concluded, and the event has justified my opinion, that these assurances had been given on the general characters of men by such of our friends as had embarked sooner and gone farther than the rest.

This management surprised me extremely. In the answers I made I endeavoured to set the mistake right, to show that things were far from the point of maturity imagined, that the Chevalier had yet no party for him, and that nothing could form one but the extreme violence which the Whigs threatened to exercise. Great endeavours were used to engage me in this affair, and to prevail on me to answer the letter of invitation sent me from Bar. I alleged, as it was true, that I had no commission from any person in England, and that the friends I left behind me were the only persons who could determine me, if any could, to take such a step. As to the last proposition, I absolutely refused it.

In the uncertainty of what would happen - whether the prosecutions would be pushed, which was most probable, in the manner intended against me, and against others, for all of whom, except the

Earl of Oxford, I had as much concern as for myself; or whether the Whigs would relent, drop some, and soften the fate of others - I resolved to conduct myself so as to create no appearance which might be strained into a pretence for hard usage, and which might be retorted on my friends when they debated for me, or when they defended themselves. I saw the Earl of Stair; I promised him that I would enter into no Jacobite engagements, and I kept my word with him. I wrote a letter to Mr. Secretary Stanhope which might take off any imputation of neglect of the Government, and I retired into Dauphine to remove the objection of residence near the Court of France.

This retreat from Paris was censured in England, and styled a desertion of my friends and of their cause, with what foundation let any reasonable man determine. Had I engaged with the Pretender before the party acted for him, or required of me that I should do so, I had taken the air of being his man; whereas I looked on myself as theirs. I had gone about to bring them into his measures; whereas I never intended, even since that time, to do anything more than to make him as far as possible act conformably to their views.

During the short time I continued on the banks of the Rhone the prosecutions were carried on at Westminster with the utmost violence, and the ferment among the people was risen to such a degree that it could end in nothing better - it might have ended in something worse - than it did. The measures which I observed at Paris had turned to no account; on the contrary, the letter which I wrote to Mr. Secretary Stanhope was quoted as a base and fawning submission, and what I intended as a mark of respect to the Government and a service to my friends was perverted to ruin me in the opinion of the latter. The Act of Attainder, in consequence of my impeachment, had passed against me for crimes of the blackest dye; and among other inducements to pass it, my having been engaged in the Pretender's interest was one. How well founded this Article was has already appeared; I was just as guilty of the rest. The correspondence with me was, you know, neither frequent nor safe. I heard seldom and darkly from you, and though I saw well enough which way the current ran, yet I was entirely ignorant of the measures you took, and of the use you intended to make of me. I contented myself, therefore, with letting you all know that you had but to command me, and that I was ready to venture in your service the little which remained, as frankly as I had exposed all which was gone. At last your commands came, and I shall show you in what manner I executed them.

The person who was sent to me arrived in the beginning of July, 1715, at the place where I was. He spoke in the name of all the friends whose authority could influence me, and he brought me word that Scotland was not only ready to take arms, but under some sort of dissatisfaction to be withheld from beginning; that in England the people were exasperated against the Government to such a degree that, far from wanting to be encouraged, they could not be restrained from insulting it on every occasion; that the whole Tory party was become avowedly Jacobite; that many officers of the army and the majority of the soldiers were very well affected to the cause; that the City of London was ready to rise; and that the enterprises for seizing of several places were ripe for execution: in a word, that most of the principal Tories were in a concert with the Duke of Ormond, for I had pressed particularly to be informed whether his Grace acted alone, or, if not, who were his council; and that the others were so disposed that there remained no doubt of their joining as soon as the first blow should be struck. He added that my friends were a little surprised to observe that I lay neuter in such a conjuncture. He represented to me the danger I ran of being prevented by people of all sides from having the merit of engaging early in this enterprise, and how unaccountable it would be for a man impeached and attainted under the present Government to take no share in bringing about a revolution so near at hand and so certain. He entreated that I would defer no longer to join the Chevalier, to advise and assist in carrying on his affairs, and to solicit and negotiate at the Court of France, where my friends imagined that I should not fail to meet with a favourable reception, and from whence they made no doubt of receiving assistance in a situation of affairs so critical, so unexpected, and so promising. He concluded by giving me a letter from the Pretender, whom he had seen in his way to me, in which I was pressed to repair without loss of time to Commercy; and this instance was grounded on the message which the bearer of the letter had brought me from my friends in England.

Since he was sent to me, it had been more proper to have come directly where I was; but he was in haste to make his own court, and to deliver the assurances which were entrusted to him. Perhaps, too, he imagined that he should tie the knot faster on me by acquainting me that my friends had actually engaged for themselves and me, than by barely telling me that they desired I would engage for myself and them.

In the progress of the conversation he related a multitude of facts which satisfied me as to the general disposition of the people; but he gave me little satisfaction as to the measures taken for improving this disposition, for driving the business on with vigour if it tended to a revolution, or for supporting it with advantage if it spun into a war. When I questioned him concerning several persons whose disinclination to the Government admitted of no doubt, and whose names, quality, and experience were very essential to the success of the undertaking, he owned to me that they kept a great reserve, and did, at most, but encourage others to act by general and dark expressions.

I received this account and this summons ill in my bed; yet, important as the matter was, a few minutes served to determine me. The circumstances wanting to form a reasonable inducement to engage did not escape me. But the smart of a Bill of Attainder tingled in every vein; and I looked on my party to be under oppression and to call for my assistance. Besides which I considered, first, that I should certainly be informed, when I conferred with the Chevalier, of many particulars unknown to this gentleman; for I did not imagine that you could be so near to take arms, as he represented you to be, on no other foundation than that which he exposed. And, secondly, that I was obliged in honour to declare, without waiting for a more particular information of what might be expected from England, since my friends had taken their resolution to declare, without any previous assurance of what might be expected from France. This second motive weighed extremely with me at that time; there is, however, more sound than sense in it, and it contains the original error to which all your subsequent errors, and the thread of misfortunes which followed, are to be ascribed.

My resolution thus taken, I lost no time in repairing to Commercy. The very first conversations with the Chevalier answered in no degree my expectations; and I assure you, with great truth, that I began even then, if not to repent of my own rashness, yet to be fully convinced both of yours and mine.

He talked to me like a man who expected every moment to set out for England or Scotland, but who did not very well know for which. And when he entered into the particulars of his affairs I found that concerning the former he had nothing more circumstantial nor positive to go upon than what I had already heard. The advices which were sent from thence contained such assurances of success as it was hard to think that men who did not go upon the surest grounds would presume to give. But then these assurances were general, and the authority seldom satisfactory. Those which came from the best hands were verbal, and often conveyed by very doubtful messengers; others came from men whose fortunes were as desperate as their counsels; and others came from persons whose situation in the world gave little reason to attend to their judgment in matters of this kind.

The Duke of Ormond had been for some time, I cannot say how long, engaged with the Chevalier. He had taken the direction of this whole affair, as far as it related to England, upon himself, and had received a commission for this purpose, which contained the most ample powers that could be given. After this, one would be apt to imagine that the principles on which the Pretender should proceed, and the Tories engage, in this service had been laid down; that a regular and certain method of correspondence had been established; that the necessary assistances had been specified; and that positive assurances had been given of them. Nothing less. In a matter as serious as this, all was loose and abandoned to the disposition of fortune. The first point had never been touched upon; by what I have said above you see how little care was taken of the second; and as to the third, the Duke had asked a small body of regular forces, a sum of money, and a quantity of arms and ammunition. He had been told in answer by the Court of France that he must absolutely despair of any number of troops whatever, but he had been made in general to hope for some money, some arms, and some ammunition; a little sum had, I think, been advanced to him. In a case so plain as this it is hard to conceive how any man could err. The assistances demanded from France at this time, and even greater than these, will appear, in the sequel of this relation, by the sense of the whole party, to have been deemed essentially necessary to success. In such an uncertainty, therefore, whether even these could be obtained, or rather with so much reason to apprehend that they could not, it was evident that the Tories ought to have lain still. They might have helped the ferment against the Government, but should have avoided with the utmost care the giving any alarm or even suspicion of their true design, and have resumed or not resumed it as the Chevalier was able or not able to provide the troops, the arms, the money, etc. Instead of which those who were at the head of the undertaking, and therefore answerable for the measures which were pursued, suffered the business to jog merrily on. They knew in general how little dependence was to be placed on foreign succour, but acted as if they had been sure of it; while the party were rendered sanguine by their passions, and made no doubt of subverting a Government they were angry with, both one and the other made as much bustle and gave as great alarm as would have been imprudent even at the eve of a general insurrection. This appeared to me to be the state of things with respect to England when I arrived at Commercy.

The Scots had long pressed the Chevalier to come amongst them, and had of late sent frequent messages to quicken his departure, some of which were delivered in terms much more zealous than respectful. The truth is, they seemed in as much haste to begin as if they had thought themselves able to do the work alone; as if they had been apprehensive of no danger but that of seeing it taken out of their hands and of having the honour of it shared by others. However, that which was wanting on the part of England was not wanting in Scotland; the Scots talked aloud, but they were in a condition to rise. They took little care to keep their intentions secret, but they were disposed to put those intentions into immediate execution, and thereby to render the secret no longer necessary. They knew upon whom to depend for every part of the work, and they had concerted with the Chevalier even to the place of his landing.

There was need of no great sagacity to perceive how unequal such foundations were to the weight of the building designed to be raised on them. The Scots, with all their zeal and all their valour, could bring no revolution about unless in concurrence with the English; and among the latter nothing was ripe for such an under-taking but the temper of the people, if that was so. I thought, there-fore, that the Pretender's friends in the North should be kept from rising till those in the South had put themselves in a condition to act; and that in the meanwhile the utmost endeavours ought to be used with the King of France to espouse the cause; and that a plan of the design, with a more particular specification of the succours desired, as well as of the time when and the place to which they should be conveyed, ought to be written for; - all which I was told by the Marshal of Berwick, who had the principal direction at that time of these affairs in France, and I daresay very truly, had been often asked, but never sent. I looked on this enterprise to be of the nature of those which can hardly be undertaken more than once, and I judged that the success of it would depend on timing as near as possible together the insurrection in both parts of the island and the succours from hence. The Pretender approved this opinion of mine. He instructed me accordingly, and I left Lorraine after having accepted the Seals much against my inclination. I made one condi-tion with him; it was this - that I should be at liberty to quit a station which my humour and many other considerations made me think myself very unfit for, whenever the occasion upon which I engaged was over, one way or other; and I desire you to remember that I did so.

I arrived at Paris towards the end of July, 1715. You will observe that all I was charged with, and all by consequence that I am an-swerable for, was to solicit this Court and to dispose them to grant us the succours necessary to make the attempt as soon as we should know certainly from England in what it was desired that these suc-cours should consist and whither they should be sent. Here I found a multitude of people at work, and every one doing what seemed good in his own eyes; no subordination, no order, no concert. Per-sons concerned in the management of these affairs upon former occasions have assured me this is always the case. It might be so to some degree, but I believe never so much as now. The Jacobites had wrought one another up to look on the success of the present designs as infallible. Every meeting-house which the populace demolished, every little drunken riot which happened, served to confirm them in these sanguine expectations; and there was hardly one amongst them who would lose the air of contributing by his intrigues to the Restoration, which, he took it for granted, would be brought about, without him, in a very few weeks.

Care and hope sat on every busy Irish face. Those who could write and read had letters to show; and those who had not arrived to this pitch of erudition had their secrets to whisper. No sex was excluded from this Ministry. Fanny Oglethorpe, whom you must have seen in England, kept her corner in it, and Olive Trant was the great wheel of our machine.

I imagine that this picture, the lines of which are not in the least too strong, would serve to represent what passed on your side of the water at the same time. The letters which came from thence seemed to me to contain rather such things as the writers wished might be true, than such as they knew to be so: and the accounts which were sent from hence were of the same kind. The vanity of some and the credulity of others supported this ridiculous correspondence; and I question not but very many persons, some such I have known, did the same thing from a principle which they took to be a very wise one: they imagined that they helped by these means to maintain and to increase the spirit of the party in England and France. They acted like Thoas, that turbulent Ftolian, who brought Antiochus into Greece: "quibus mendaciis de rege, multiplicando verbis copias ejus, erexerat multorum in Graecia animos; iisdem et regis spem inflabat, omnium votis eum arcessi." Thus were numbers of people employed under a notion of advancing the business, or from an affectation of importance, in amusing and flattering one another and in sounding the alarm in the ears of an enemy whom it was their interest to surprise. The Government of England was put on its guard: and the necessity of acting, or of laying aside with some disadvantage all thoughts of acting for the present, was precipitated before any measures necessary to enable you to act had been prepared, or almost thought of.

If his Majesty did not, till some short time after this, declare the intended invasion to Parliament it was not for want of information. Before I came to Paris, what was doing had been discovered. The little armament made at the Havre, which furnished the only means the Chevalier then had for his transportation into Britain, which had exhausted the treasury of St. Germains, and which contained all the arms and ammunition that could be depended upon for the whole undertaking, though they were hardly sufficient to begin the work even in Scotland, was talked of publicly. A Minister less alert and less capable than the Earl of Stair would easily have been at the bottom of the secret, for so it was called, when the particulars of messages received and sent, the names of the persons from whom they came, and by whom they were carried, were whispered about at tea-tables and in coffee-houses.

In short, what by the indiscretion of people here, what by the re-bound which came often back from London, what by the private interests and ambitious views of persons in the French Court, and what by other causes unnecessary to be examined now, the most private transactions came to light: and they who imagined that they trusted their heads to the keeping of one or two friends, were in reality at the mercy of numbers. Into such company was I fallen for my sins; and it is upon the credit of such a mob Ministry that the Tories have judged me capable of betraying a trust, or incapable of discharging it.

I had made very little progress in the business which brought me to Paris, when the paper so long expected was sent, in pursuance of former instances, from England. The unanimous sense of the principal persons engaged was contained in it. The whole had been dictated word for word to the gentleman who brought it over, by the Earl of Mar, and it had been delivered to him by the Duke of Ormond. I was driving in the wide ocean without a compass when this dropped unexpectedly into my hands. I received it joyfully, and I steered my course exactly by it. Whether the persons from whom it came pursued the principles and observed the rules which they laid down as the measures of their own conduct and of ours, will appear by the sequel of this relation.

This memorial asserted that there were no hopes of succeeding in a present undertaking, for many reasons deduced in it, without an immediate and universal rising of the people in all parts of England upon the Chevalier's arrival; and that this insurrection was in no degree probable unless he brought a body of regular troops along with him: that if this attempt miscarried, his cause and his friends, the English liberty and Government, would be utterly ruined: but if by coming without troops he resolved to risk these and everything else, he must set out so as not to arrive before the end of September, to justify which opinion many arguments were urged. In this case twenty thousand arms, a train of artillery, five hundred officers with their servants, and a considerable sum of money were demanded: and as soon as they should be informed that the Chevalier was in condition to make this provision, it was said that notice should be given him of the places to which he might send, and of the persons who were to be trusted. I do not mention some inconveniences which they touched upon arising from a delay; because their opinion was clearly for this delay, and because that they could not suppose that the Chevalier would act, or that those about him would advise him to act, contrary to the sense of all his friends in England. No time was lost in making the proper use of this paper. As much of it as was fit to be shown to this Court was translated into French, and laid before the King of France. I was now able to speak with greater assurance, and in some sort to undertake conditionally for the event of things.

The proposal of violating treaties so lately and so solemnly concluded, was a very bold one to be made to people, whatever their inclinations might be, whom the war had reduced to the lowest ebb of riches and power. They would not hear of a direct and open engagement, such as the sending a body of troops would have been; neither would they grant the whole of what was asked in the second plan. But it was impossible for them, or any one else, to foresee how far those steps which they were willing to take, well improved, might have encouraged or forced them to go. They granted us some succours, and the very ship in which the Pretender was to transport himself was fitted out by Depine d'Anicant at the King of France's expense. They would have concealed these appearances as much as they could; but the heat of the Whigs and the resentment of the

Court of England might have drawn them in. We should have been glad indirectly to concur in fixing these things upon them: and, in a word, if the late King had lived six months longer, I verily believe there had been war again between England and France. This was the only point of time when these affairs had, to my apprehension, the least reasonable appearance even of possibility: all that preceded was wild and uncertain: all that followed was mad and desperate. But this favourable aspect had an extreme short duration. Two events soon happened, one of which cast a damp on all we were doing, and the other rendered vain and fruitless all we had done. The first was the arrival of the Duke of Ormond in France, the other was the death of the King.

We had sounded the duke's name high. His reputation and the opinion of his power were great. The French began to believe that he was able to form and to head a party; that the troops would join him; that the nation would follow the signal whenever he drew his sword; and the voice of the people, the echo of which was continually in their ears, confirmed them in this belief. But when, in the midst of all these bright ideas, they saw him arrive, almost literally alone, when, to excuse his coming, I was obliged to tell them that he could not stay, they sank at once from their hopes, and that which generally happens happened in this case: because they had had too good an opinion of the cause, they began to form too bad a one. Before this time, if they had no friendship for the Tories, they had at least some consideration and esteem. After this, I saw nothing but compassion in the best of them, and contempt in the others.

When I arrived at Paris, the King was already gone to Marly, where the indisposition which he had begun to feel at Versailles increased upon him. He was the best friend the Chevalier had: and when I engaged in this business, my principal dependence was on his personal character. This failed me to a great degree; he was not in a condition to exert the same vigour as formerly. The Ministers who saw so great an event as his death to be probably at hand, a certain minority, an uncertain regency, perhaps confusion, at best a new face of Government and a new system of affairs, would not, for their own sakes, as well as for the sake of the public, venture to engage far in any new measures. All I had to negotiate by myself first, and in conjunction with the Duke of Ormond soon afterwards, languished with the King. My hopes sank as he declined, and died when he expired. The event of things has sufficiently shown that all those which were entertained by the duke and the Jacobite party under the Regency, were founded on the grossest delusions imaginable. Thus was the project become impracticable before the time arrived which was fixed by those who directed things in England for putting it in execution.

The new Government of France appeared to me like a strange country. I was little acquainted with the roads. Most of the faces I met with were unknown to me, and I hardly understood the language of the people. Of the men who had been in power under the late reign, many were discarded, and most of the others were too much taken up with the thoughts of securing themselves under this, to receive applications in favour of the Pretender. The two men who had the greatest appearance of favour and power were D'Aguesseau and Noailles. One was made Chancellor, on the death of Voisin, from Attorney-General; and the other was placed at the head of the Treasury. The first passes for a man of parts, but he never acted out of the sphere of the law: I had no acquaintance with him before this time; and when you consider his circumstances and mine, you will not think it could be very easy for me to get access to him now. The latter I had known extremely well whilst the late King lived: and from the same Court principle, as he was glad to be well with me then, he would hardly know me now. The Minister who had the principal direction of foreign affairs I lived in friendship with, and I must own, to his honour, that he never encouraged a design which he knew that his Court had no intention of supporting.

There were other persons, not to tire you with farther particulars upon this head, of credit and influence with whom I found indirect and private ways of conversing; but it was in vain to expect any more than civil language from them in a case which they found no disposition in their Master to countenance, and in favour of which they had no prejudices of their own. The private engagements into which the Duke of Orleans had entered with his Majesty during the life of the late King will abate of their force as the Regent grows into strength, and would soon have had no force at all if the Pretender had met with success: but in these beginnings they operated very strongly. The air of this Court was to take the counterpart of all which had been thought right under Louis XIV. "Cela resemble trop ` l'ancien systhme" was an answer so often given that it became a jest and almost a proverb. But to finish this account with a fact which is incredible, but strictly true; the very peace which had saved France from ruin, and the makers of it, were become as unpopular at this Court as at the Court of Vienna.

The Duke of Ormond flattered himself, in this state of things, that he had opened a private and sure channel of arriving at the Regent, and of bending him to his purposes. His Grace and I lived together at this time in an house which one of my friends had lent me. I observed that he was frequently lost, and that he made continual excursions out of town, with all the mysterious precaution imaginable. I doubted at first whether those intrigues related to business or pleasure. I soon discovered with whom they were carried on, and had reason to believe that both were mingled in them. It is necessary that I explain this secret to you.

Mrs. Trant, whom I have named above, had been preparing herself for the retired abstemious life of a Carmelite by taking a surfeit of the pleasures of Paris, when, a little before the death of the Queen, or about that time, she went into England. What she was entrusted either by the Chevalier, or any other person, to negotiate there, I am ignorant of; and it imports not much to know. In that journey she made or renewed an acquaintance with the Duke of Ormond. The scandalous chronicle affirms that she brought with her, when she returned into France, a woman of whom I have not the least knowledge, but who was probably handsome, since without beauty such a merchandise would not have been saleable, nor have answered the design of the importer; and that she made this way her court to the Regent. Whatever her merit was, she kept a correspondence with him, and put herself upon that foot of familiarity which he permits all those who contribute to his pleasures to assume. She was placed by him, as she told me herself, where I found her some time after that which I am speaking of, in the house of an ancient gentlewoman who had formerly been Maid of Honour to Madame, and who had contracted at Court a spirit of intrigue which accompanied her in her retreat.

These two had associated to them the Abbi de Tesieu in all the political parts of their business; for I will not suppose that so reverend an ecclesiastic entered into any other secret. This Abbi is the Regent's secretary; and it was chiefly through him that the private treaty had been carried on between his master and the Earl of Stair in the King's reign. Whether the priest had stooped at the lure of a cardinal's hat, or whether he acted the second part by the same orders that he acted the first, I know not. This is sure, and the British Minister was not the bubble of it - that whilst he concerted measures on one hand to traverse the Pretender's designs, he testified on the other all the inclination possible to his service. A mad fellow who had been an intendant in Normandy, and several other politicians of the lowest form, were at different times taken into this famous Junto.

With these worthy people his Grace of Ormond negotiated; and no care was omitted on his part to keep me out of the secret. The reason of which, as far as I am able to guess at, shall be explained to you by-and-by. I might very justly have taken this proceeding ill, and the duke will not be able to find in my whole conduct towards him anything like it; I protest to you very sincerely I was not in the least moved at it.

He advanced not a step in his business with these sham Ministers, and yet imagined that he got daily ground. I made no progress with the true ones, but I saw it. These, however, were not our only difficulties. We lay under another, which came from your side, and which embarrassed us more. The first hindered us from working forward to our point of view, but the second took all point of view from us.

A paper was sent into England just before the death of the King of France, which had been drawn by me at Chaville in concert with the Dukes of Ormond and Berwick, and with Monsieur de Torcy. This paper was an answer to the memorial received from thence. The state of this country was truly represented in it: the difference was fixed between what had been asked, and what might be expected from France; and upon the whole it was demanded what our friends would do, and what they would have us to do. The reply to this came through the French Secretary of State to our hands. They declared themselves unable to say anything till they should see what turn affairs would take on so great an event as the death of the King, the report of which had reached them.

Such a declaration shut our mouths and tied our hands. I confess I knew neither how to solicit, nor what to solicit; this last message suspending the project on which we had acted before, and which I kept as an instruction constantly before my eyes. It seemed to me uncertain whether you intended to go on, or whether your design was to stifle, as much as possible, all past transactions; to lie perfectly still; to throw upon the Court the odium of having given a false alarm; and to wait till new accidents at home, and a more favourable conjuncture abroad, might tempt you to resume the enterprise. Perhaps this would have been the wisest game you could have played: but then you should have concerted it with us who acted for you here. You intended no such thing, as appeared afterwards: and therefore those who acted for the party at London, whoever they were, must be deemed inexcusable for leaving things on the foot of this message, and giving us no advice fit to be depended upon for many weeks. Whilst preparations were to be made, and the work was to be set a-going by assistance from hence, you might reasonably expect to hear from us, and to be determined by us: but when all hopes of this kind seemed to be gone, it was your part to determine us; and we could take no resolution here but that of conforming ourselves to whatever should come prescribed from England.

Whilst we were in this condition, the most desperate that can be imagined, we began to receive verbal messages from you that no more time was to be lost, and that the Chevalier should come away. No man was, I believe, ever so embarrassed as I found myself at that time. I could not imagine that you would content yourselves by loose verbal messages, after all that had happened, to call us over; and I knew by experience how little such messages are to be depended on. For soon after I engaged in these affairs, a monk arrived at Bar, despatched, as he affirmed, by the Duke of Ormond, in whose name he insisted that the Chevalier should hasten into Britain, and that nothing but his presence was wanting to place the crown on his head. The fellow delivered his errand so positively, and so circumstantially, that the resolution was taken at Bar to set out, and my rendezvous to join the Chevalier was appointed me. This method to fetch a King, with as little ceremony as one would invite a friend to supper, appeared somewhat odd to me, who was then very new in these affairs. But when I came to talk with the man, for by good luck he had been sent for from Bar to Paris, I easily discerned that he had no such commission as he pretended to, and that he acted of his own head. I presumed to oppose the taking any resolution upon his word, though he was a monk: and soon after we knew from the Duke of Ormond himself that he had never sent him.

This example made me cautious; but that which determined my opinion was, that I could never imagine, without supposing you all run mad, that the same men who judged this attempt unripe for execution, unless supported by regular troops from France, or at least by all the other assistances which are enumerated above, while the design was much more secret than at present; when the King had no fleet at sea, nor more than eight thousand men dispersed over the whole island; when we had the good wishes of the French Court on our side, and were sure of some particular assistances, and of a general connivance; that the same men, I say, should press for making it now without any other preparation, when we had neither money, arms, ammunition, nor a single company of foot; when the Government of England was on its guard, national troops were raised, foreign forces sent for, and France, like all the rest of the Continent, against us. I could not conceive such a strange combination of accidents as should make the necessity of acting increase gradually upon us as the means of doing so were taken from us.

Upon the whole matter, my opinion was, and I did not observe the Duke of Ormond to differ from me, that we should wait till we heard from you in such a manner as might assure us of what you intended to do yourselves, and of what you expected from us; and that in the meanwhile we should go as far as the little money which we had, and the little favour which was shown us would allow, in getting some embarkations ready on the coast.

Sir George Byng had come into the road of Havre, and had demanded by name several ships which belonged to us to be given up to him. The Regent did not think fit to let him have the ships; but he ordered them to be unloaded, and their cargoes were put into the King's magazines. We were in no condition to repair the loss; and therefore when I mention embarkations, you will please to understand nothing more than vessels to transport the Pretender's person and the persons of those who should go over with him. This was all we could do, and this was not neglected.

We were thus employed when a gentleman arrived from Scotland to represent the state of that country, and to require a definitive answer from the Chevalier whether he would have the insurrection to be made immediately, which they apprehended they might not be able to make at all if they were obliged to defer it much longer. This gentleman was sent instantly back again, and was directed to let the persons he came from know that the Chevalier was desirous to have the rising of his friends in England and Scotland so adjusted that they might mutually assist each other and distract the enemy; that he had not received a final answer from his friends in England, but that he was in daily expectation of it; that it was very much to be wished that all attempts in Scotland could be suspended till such time as the English were ready; but that if the Scots were so pressed that they must either submit or rise immediately, he was of opinion they should rise, and he would make the best of his way to them.

What this forwardness in the Scots and this uncertainty and backwardness in the English must produce, it was not hard to foresee; and, therefore, that I might neglect nothing in my power to prevent any false measures - as I was conscious to myself that I had neglected nothing to promote true ones - I despatched a gentleman to London, where I supposed the Earl of Mar to be, some days before the message I have just spoken of was sent to Scotland. I desired him to make my compliments to Lord Mar, and to tell him from me that I understood it to be his sense, as well as the sense of all our friends, that Scotland could do nothing effectually without the concurrence of England, and that England would not stir without assistance from abroad; that he might assure himself no such assistance could be depended upon; and that I begged of him to make the inference from these propositions. The gentleman went; but upon his arrival at London he found that the Earl of Mar was already set out to draw the Highlanders into arms. He communicated his message to a person of confidence, who undertook to send it after his lordship; and this was the utmost which either he or I could do in such a conjuncture.

You were now visibly departed from the very scheme which you had sent us over, and from all the principles which had been ever laid down. I did what I could to keep up my own spirit, as well as the spirits of the Chevalier, and of all those with whom I was in correspondence: I endeavoured even to deceive myself. I could not remedy the mischief, and I was resolved to see the conclusion of the perilous adventure; but I own to you that I thought then, and that I have not changed my opinion since, that such measures as these would not be pursued by any reasonable man in the most common affairs of life. It was with the utmost astonishment that I saw them pursued in the conduct of an enterprise which had for its object nothing less than the disposition of crowns, and for the means of bringing it about nothing less than a civil war.

Impatient that we heard nothing from England, when we expected every moment to hear that the war was begun in Scotland, the Duke of Ormond and I resolved to send a person of confidence to London. We instructed him to repeat to you the former accounts which we had sent over, to let you know how destitute the Chevalier was either of actual support or even of reasonable hopes, and to desire that you would determine whether he should go to Scotland or throw himself on some part of the English coast. This person was further instructed to tell you that, the Chevalier being ready to take any resolution at a moment's warning, you might depend on his setting out the instant he received your answer; and, therefore, that to save time, if your intention was to rise, you would do well to act immediately, on the assurance that the plan you prescribed, be it what it would, should be exactly complied with. We took this resolution the rather because one of the packets, which had been prepared in cypher to give you an account of things, which had been put above three weeks before into Monsieur de Torcy's hands, and which by consequence we thought to be in yours, was by this time sent back to me by this Minister (I think, open), with an excuse that he durst not take upon him to forward it.

The person despatched to London returned very soon to us, and the answer he brought was, that since affairs grew daily worse, and could not mend by delay, our friends in England had resolved to declare immediately, and that they would be ready to join the Chevalier on his landing; that his person would be as safe there as in Scotland, and that in every other respect it was better that he should land in England; that they had used their utmost endeavours, and that they hoped the western counties were in a good posture to receive him. To this was added a general indication of the place he should come to, as near to Plymouth as possible.

You must agree that this was not the answer of men who knew what they were about. A little more precision was necessary in dictating a message which was to have such consequences, and especially since the gentleman could not fail to acquaint the persons he spoke with that the Chevalier was not able to carry men enough to secure him from being taken up even by the first constable. Notwithstanding this, the Duke of Ormond set out from Paris and the Chevalier from Bar. Some persons were sent to the North of England and others to London to give notice that they were both on their way. Their routes were so ordered that the Duke of Ormond was to sail from the coast of Normandy some days before the Chevalier arrived at St. Malo, to which place the duke was to send immediate notice of his landing; and two gentlemen acquainted with the country, and perfectly well known to all our friends in those parts, were despatched before, that the people of Devonshire and Somersetshire, who were, we concluded, in arms, might be apprised of the signals which were to be made from the ships, and might be ready to receive the duke.

On the coast of France, and before his embarkation, the duke heard that several of our principal friends had been seized immediately after the person who came last from them had left London, that the others were all dispersed, and that the consternation was universal. He embarked, notwithstanding this melancholy news, and, sup-

ported by nothing but the firmness of his temper, he went over to
the place appointed; he did more than his part, and he found that
our friends had done less than theirs. One of the gentlemen who
had passed over before him, and had traversed part of the country,
joined him on the coast, and assured him that there was not the
least room to expect a rising; in a word, he was refused a night's
lodging in a country which we had been told was in a good posture
to receive the Chevalier, and where the duke expected that multitudes would repair to him.

He returned to the coast of Brittany after this uncomfortable expedition, where the Chevalier arrived about the same time from Lorraine. What his Grace proposed by the second attempt, which he
made as soon as the vessel could be refitted, to land in the same part
of the island, I profess myself to be ignorant. I wrote him my opinion at the time, and I have always thought that the storm in which
he had like to have been cast away, and which forced him back to
the French coast, saved him from a much greater peril - that of per-
ishing in an attempt as full of extravagant rashness, and as void of
all reasonable meaning, as any of those adventures which have
rendered the hero of La Mancha immortal.

The Chevalier had now but one of these two things left him to do:
one was to return to Bar; the other was to go to Scotland, where
there were people in arms for him. He took this last resolution. He
left Brittany, where he had as many Ministers as there were people
about him, and where he was eternally teased with noisy disputes
about what was to be done in circumstances in which no reasonable
thing could be done. He sent to have a vessel got ready for him at
Dunkirk, and he crossed the country as privately as he could.

Whilst all these things passed I remained at Paris to try if by any
means some assistance might be at last procured, without which it
was evident, even to those who flattered themselves the most, that
the game was up.

No sooner was the Duke of Ormond gone from Paris on the design
which I have mentioned, and Mrs. Trant, who had accompanied
him part of the way, returned, but I was sent for to a little house at

Madrid, in the Bois de Boulogne, where she lived with Mademoiselle de Chaussery, the ancient gentlewoman with whom the Duke of Orleans had placed her. These two persons opened to me what had passed whilst the Duke of Ormond was here, and the hopes they had of drawing the Regent into all the measures necessary to support the attempts which were making in favour of the Chevalier.

By what they told me at first I saw that they had been trusted, and by what passed in the course of my treating with them it appeared that they had the access which they pretended to. All which I had been able to do by proper persons and in proper methods, since the King of France's death, amounting to little or nothing, I resolved, at last, to try what was to be done by this indirect way. I put myself under the conduct of these female managers, and without having the same dependence on them as his Grace of Ormond had, I pushed their credit and their power as far as they reached during the time I continued to see them. I met with smoother language and greater hopes than had been given me hitherto. A note signed by the Regent, supposed to be written to a woman, but which was to be explained to be intended for the Earl of Mar, was put into my hands to be sent to Scotland. I took a copy of it, which you may see at the end of these papers. When Sir John Areskine came to press for succour, the Regent was prevailed upon by these women to see him; but he carried nothing real back with him except a quantity of gold, part of the money which we had drawn from Spain, and which was lost, with the vessel, in a very odd manner, on the Scotch coast. The Duke of Ormond had been promised seven or eight thousand arms, which were drawn out of the magazines, and said to be lodged, I think, at Compihgne. I used my utmost efforts that these arms might be carried forward to the coast, and I undertook for their transportation, but all was in vain, so that the likelihood of bringing anything to effect in time appeared to me no greater than I had found it before I entered into this intrigue.

I soon grew tired of a commerce which nothing but success could render tolerable, and resolved to be no longer amused by the pretences which were daily repeated to me, that the Regent had entertained personal prejudices against me, and that he was insensibly and by degrees to be dipped in our measures; that both these things required time, but that they would certainly be brought about, and that we should then be able to answer all the expectations of the English and the Scotch. The first of these pretences contained a fact which I could hardly persuade myself to be true, because I knew very certainly that I had never given His Royal Highness the least occasion for such prejudices; the second was a work which might spin out into a great and uncertain length. I took my resolution to drive what related to myself to an immediate explanation, and what related to others to an immediate decision; not to suffer any excuse for doing nothing to be founded on my conduct, nor the salvation, if I could hinder it, of so many gallant men as were in arms in Scotland, to rest on the success of such womanish projects. I shall tell you what I did on the first head now, and what I did on the second, hereafter, in its proper place.

The fact which it was said the Regent laid to my charge was a correspondence with Lord Stair, and having been one night at his house from whence I did not retire till three in the morning. As soon as I got hold of this I desired the Marshal of Berwick to go to him. The Marshal told him, from me, that I had been extremely concerned to hear in general that I lay under his displeasure; that a story, which it was said he believed, had been related to me; that I expected the justice, which he could deny to no man, of having the accusation proved, in which case I was contented to pass for the last of humankind, or of being justified if it could not be proved. He answered that such a story had been related to him by such persons as he thought would not have deceived him; that he had been since convinced that it was false, and that I should be satisfied of his regard for me; but that he must own he was very uneasy to find that I, who could apply to him through the Marshal d'Huxelles, could choose to treat with Mrs. Trant and the rest; for he named all the cabal, except his secretary, whom I had never met at Mademoiselle Chaussery's. He added that these people teased him, at my instigation, to death, and that they were not fit to be trusted with any business. He applied to some of them the severest epithets. The Marshal of Berwick replied that he was sure I should receive the whole of what he had been pleased to say with the greatest satisfaction; that I had treated with those persons much against my will; and, finally, that if his Royal Highness would not employ them he was sure I would never apply to them. In a conversation which I had not long after with him he spoke to me in much the same terms as he had done to the Marshal. I went from him very ill edified as to his intentions of doing anything in favour of the Chevalier; but I carried away with me this satisfaction, that he had assigned me, from his own mouth, the person through whom I should make my applications to him, and through whom I should depend on receiving his answers; that he had disavowed all the little politic clubs, and had commanded me to have no more to do with them.

Before I resume the thread of my narration give me leave to make some reflection upon what I have been last saying to you. When I met with the Duke of Ormond at his return from the coast, he thought himself obliged to say something to excuse his keeping me out of a secret which during his absence I had been let into. His excuse was that the Regent had exacted from him that I should know nothing of the matter. You will observe that the account which I have given you seems to contradict this assertion of his Grace, since it is hard to suppose that if the Regent had exacted that I should be kept out of the secret, these women would have dared to have let me into it, and since it is still harder to suppose that the Regent would make this express condition with the Duke of Ormond, and the moment the duke's back was turned would suffer these women to tease him from me and to bring me answers from him. I am, however, far from taxing the duke with affirming an untruth. I believe the Regent did make such a condition with him; and I will tell you how I understand all this little management, which will explain a great deal to you. This Prince, with wit and valour, has joined all the irresolution of temper possible, and is, perhaps, the man in the world the least capable of saying "no" to your face. From hence it happened that these women, like multitudes of other people, forced him to say and do enough to give them the air of having credit with him and of being trusted by him. This drew in the Duke of Ormond, who is not, I daresay, as yet undeceived. The Regent never intended from the first to do anything, even indirectly, in favour of the Jacobite cause. His interest was plainly on the other side, and he saw it. But then the same weakness in his character carried him, as it would have done his great-uncle Gaston in the same case, to keep measures with the

Chevalier. His double-trimming character prevailed on him to talk with the Duke of Ormond, but it carried him no farther. I question not but he did, on this occasion, what you must have observed many men to do: we not only endeavour to impose on the world, but even on ourselves; we disguise our weakness, and work up in our minds an opinion that the measure which we fall into by the natural or habitual imperfection of our character is the effect of a principle of prudence or of some other virtue. Thus the Regent, who saw the Duke of Ormond because he could not resist the importunity of Olive Trant, and who gave hopes to the duke because he can refuse nobody, made himself believe that it was a great strain of policy to blow up the fire and to keep Britain embroiled. I am persuaded that I do not err in judging that he thought in this manner, and here I fix the reason of his excluding me out of the commerce which he had with the Duke of Ormond, of his affecting a personal dislike of me, and of his avoiding any correspondence with me upon these matters, till I forced myself in a manner upon him, and he could not keep me any longer at a distance without departing from his first principle - that of keeping measures with everybody. He then threw me, or let me slide if you will, into the hands of these women; and when he found that I pressed him hard that way, too, he took me out of their hands and put me back again into the proper channel of business, where I had not been long, as you will see by-and-by, before the scene of amusement was finished.

Sir John Areskine told me when he came from the first audience that he had of his Royal Highness, that he put him in mind of the encouragement which he had given the Earl of Mar to take arms. I never heard anything of this kind but what Sir John let drop to me. If the fact be true, you see that the Scotch general had been amused by him with a witness. The English general was so in his turn; and while this was doing, the Regent might think it best to have him to himself. Four eyes comprehend more objects than two, and I was a little better acquainted with the characters of people, and the mass of the country, than the duke, though this Court had been at first a strange country to me in comparison of the former.

An infinity of little circumstances concurred to make me form this opinion, some of which are better felt than explained, and many of which are not present to my memory. That which had the greatest weight with me, and which is, I think, decisive, I will mention. At the very time when it is pretended that the Regent treated with the Duke of Ormond on the express condition that I should know nothing of the matter, two persons of the first rank and greatest credit in this Court, when I made the most pressing instances to them in favour of the Chevalier, threw out in conversation to me that I should attach myself to the Duke of Orleans, that in my circumstances I might want him, and that he might have occasion for me. Something was intimated of pensions and establishment, and of making my peace at home. I would not understand this language, because I would not break with the people who held it: and when they saw that I would not take the hints, they ceased to give them.

I fancy that you see by this time the motives of the Regent's conduct. I am not, I confess, able to explain to you those of the Duke of Ormond's; I cannot so much as guess at them. When he came into France, I was careful to show him all the friendship and all the respect possible. My friends were his, my purse was his, and even my bed was his. I went further; I did all those things which touch most sensibly people who have been used to pomp. I made my court to him, and haunted his levee with assiduity. In return to this behaviour - which was the pure effect of my goodwill, and which no duty that I owed his Grace, no obligation that I had to him, imposed upon me - I have great reason to suspect that he went at least half way in all which was said or done against me. He threw himself blindly into the snare which was laid for him; and instead of hindering, as he and I in concert might have done, those affairs from languishing in the manner they did several months, he furnished this Court with an excuse for not treating with me, till it was too late to play even a saving game; and he neither drove the Regent to assist the Chevalier, nor to declare that he would not assist him; though it was fatal to the cause in general, and to the Scotch in particular, not to bring one of the two about.

It was Christmas 1715 before the Chevalier sailed for Scotland. The battle of Dunblain had been fought, the business of Preston was over: there remained not the least room to expect any commotion in his favour among the English; and many of the Scotch who had declared for him began to grow cool in the cause. No prospect of success could engage him in this expedition: but it was become necessary for his reputation. The Scotch on one side spared not to reproach him, I think unjustly, for his delay; and the French on the other were extremely eager to have him gone. Some of those who knew little of British affairs imagined that his presence would produce miraculous effects. You must not be surprised at this. As near neighbours as we are, ninety-nine in an hundred among the French are as little acquainted with the inside of our island as with that of Japan. Others of them were uneasy to see him skulking about in France, and to be told of it every hour by the Earl of Stair. Others, again, imagined that he might do their business by going into Scotland, though he should not do his own: this is, they flattered themselves that he might keep a war for some time alive, which would employ the whole attention of our Government; and for the event of which they had very little concern. Unable from their natural temper, as well as their habits, to be true to any principle, they thought and acted in this manner, whilst they affected the greatest friendship to the King, and whilst they really did desire to enter into new and more intimate engagements with him. Whilst the Pretender continued in France they could neither avow him, nor favour his cause: if he once set his foot on Scotch ground, they gave hopes of indirect assistance; and if he could maintain himself in any corner of the island, they could look upon him, it was said, as a king. This was their language to us. To the British Minister they denied, they forswore, they renounced; and yet the man of the best head in all their councils, being asked by Lord Stair what they intended to do, answered, before he was aware, that they pretended to be neuters. I leave you to judge how this slip was taken up.

As soon as I received advice that the Chevalier was sailed from Dunkirk, I renewed, I redoubled all my applications. I neglected no means, I forgot no argument which my understanding could suggest to me. What the Duke of Ormond rested upon, you have seen already. And I doubt very much whether Lord Mar, if he had been here in my place, would have been able to employ measures more effectual than those which I made use of. I may, without any imputation of arrogance, compare myself on this occasion with his lordship, since there was nothing in the management of this affair above my degree of capacity; nothing equal, either in extent or difficulty, to the business which he was a spectator of, and which I carried on when we were Secretaries of State together under the late Queen.

The King of France, who was not able to furnish the Pretender with money himself, had written some time before his death to his grandson, and had obtained a promise of four hundred thousand crowns from the King of Spain. A small part of this sum had been received by the Queen's Treasurer at St. Germains, and had been either sent to Scotland or employed to defray the expenses which were daily making on the coast. I pressed the Spanish Ambassador at Paris; I solicited, by Lawless, Alberoni at Madrid, and I found another more private and more promising way of applying to him. I took care to have a number of officers picked out of the Irish troops which serve in that country; their routes were given them, and I sent a ship to receive and transport them. The money came in so slowly and in such trifling sums that it turned to little account, and the officers were on their way when the Chevalier returned from Scotland.

In the summer endeavours had been used to prevail on the King of Sweden to transport from Gottenburg the troops he had in that neighbourhood into Scotland or into the North of England. He had excused himself, not because he disliked the proposition, which, on the contrary, he thought agreeable to his interest, but for reasons of another kind. First, because the troops at hand for this service consisted in horse, not in foot, which had been asked, and which were alone proper for such an expedition. Secondly, because a declaration of this sort might turn the Protestant princes of the Empire, from whose offices he had still some prospect of assistance, against him. And thirdly, because although he knew that the King of Great Britain was his enemy, yet they were not in war together, nor had the latter acted yet awhile openly enough against him to justify such a rupture. At the time I am speaking of, these reasons were removed by the King of Sweden's being beat out of the Empire by the little consequence which his management of the Protestant princes was to him, and by the declaration of war which the King, as Elector of Hanover, made. I took up this negotiation therefore again. The Regent appeared to come into it. He spoke fair to the Baron de Spar, who pressed him on his side as I pressed him on mine, and promised, besides the arrears of the subsidy due to the Swedes, an immediate advance of fifty thousand crowns for the enterprise on Britain. He kept the officer who was to be despatched I know not how long booted; sometimes on pretence that in the low state of his credit he could not find bills of exchange for the sum, and sometimes on other pretences, and by these delays he evaded his promise. The French were very frank in declaring that they could give us no money, and that they would give us no troops. Arms, ammunition, and connivance they made us hope for. The latter, in some degree, we might have had perhaps; but to what purpose was it to connive, when by a multitude of little tricks they avoided furnishing us with arms and ammunition, and when they knew that we were utterly unable to furnish ourselves with them? I had formed the design of engaging French privateers in the Pretender's service. They were to have carried whatever we should have had to send to any part of Britain in their first voyage, and after that to have cruised under his commission. I had actually agreed for some, and it was in my power to have made the same bargains with others. Sweden on one side and Scotland on the other would have afforded them retreats. And if the war had been kept up in any part of the mountains, I conceive the execution of this design would have been of the greatest advantage to the Pretender. It failed because no other part of the work went on. He was not above six weeks in his Scotch expedition, and these were the things I endeavoured to bring to bear in his absence. I had no great opinion of my success before he went; but when he had made the last step which it was in his power to make, I resolved to suffer neither him nor the Scotch to be any longer bubbles of their own credulity and of the scandalous artifice of this Court. It would be tedious to enter into a longer narrative of all the useless pains I took. To conclude, therefore; in a conversation which I had with the M. d'Huxelles, I took occasion to declare that I would not be the instrument of amusing the Scotch, and that, since I was able to do them no other service, I would at least inform them that they must flatter themselves no longer with hopes of succour from France. I added that I would send them vessels which, with those already on the coast of Scotland, might serve to bring off the Pretender, the Earl of Mar, and as many others as possible. The Marshal approved my resolution, and advised me to execute it as the only thing which was left to do. On this occasion he showed no reserve, he was very explicit; and yet in this very point of time the promise of an order was obtained, or pretended to be obtained, from the Regent for delivering those stores of arms and ammunition which belonged to the Chevalier, and which had been put into the French magazines when Sir George Byng came to Havre. Castel Blanco is a Spaniard who married a daughter of Lord Melford, and who under that title set up for a meddler in English business. I cannot justly tell whether the honour of obtaining this promise was ascribed to him, to the Junto in the Bois de Boulogne, or to any one else. I suppose they all assumed a share of the merit. The project was that these stores should be delivered to Castel Blanco; that he should enter into a recognisance to carry them to Spain, and from thence to the West Indies; that I should provide a vessel for this purpose, which he should appear to hire or buy; and that when she was at sea she should sail directly for Scotland. You cannot believe that I reckoned much on the effect of this order, but accustomed to concur in measures the inutility of which I saw evidently enough, I concurred in this likewise. The necessary care was taken, and in a fortnight's time the ship was ready to sail, and no suspicion of her belonging to the Chevalier or of her destination was gone abroad.

As this event made no alteration in my opinion, it made none in the despatches which I prepared and sent to Scotland. In them I gave an account of what was in negotiation. I explained to him what might be hoped for in time if he was able to maintain himself in the mountains without the succours he demanded from France. But from France I told him plainly that it was in vain to expect the least part of them. In short, I concealed nothing from him. This was all I could do to put the Chevalier and his council in a condition to judge what measures to take; but these despatches never came to his hands. He was sailed from Scotland just before the gentleman whom I sent arrived on the coast. He landed at Graveline about the 22nd of February, and the first orders he gave were to stop all the vessels which were going on his account to the country from whence he came.

I saw him the morning after his arrival at St. Germains, and he received me with open arms. I had been, as soon as we heard of his return, to acquaint the French Court with it. They were not a little uneasy; and the first thing which the M. d'Huxelles said to me upon it was that the Chevalier ought to proceed to Bar with all the diligence possible, and to take possession of his former asylum before the Duke of Lorraine had time to desire him to look out for a residence somewhere else. Nothing more was meant by this proposal than to get him out of the dominions of France immediately. I was not in my mind averse to it for other reasons. Nothing could be more disadvantageous to him than to be obliged to pass the Alps, or to reside in the Papal territory on this side of them. Avignon was already named for his retreat in common conversation, and I know not whether from the time he left Scotland he ever thought of any other. I imagined that by surprising the Duke of Lorraine we should furnish that Prince with an excuse to the King and to the Emperor; that we might draw the matter into length, and gain time to negotiate some other retreat than that of Avignon for the Chevalier. The duke's goodwill there was no room to doubt of, and by what the Prince of Vaudemont told me at Paris some time afterwards I am apt to think we should have succeeded. In all events, it could not be wrong to try every measure, and the Pretender would have gone to Avignon with much better grace when he had done, in the sight of the world, all he could to avoid it.

I found him in no disposition to make such haste; he had a mind, on the contrary, to stay some time at St. Germains, and in the neighbourhood of Paris, and to have a private meeting with the Regent. He sent me back to Paris to solicit this meeting. I wrote, I spoke, to the Marshal d'Huxelles; I did my best to serve him in his own way. The Marshal answered me by word of mouth and by letter; he refused me by both. I remember he added this circumstance: that he found the Regent in bed, and acquainted him with what the Chevalier desired; that the Regent rose up in a passion, said that the things which were asked were puerilities, and swore that he would not see him. I returned without having been able to succeed in my commission; and I confess I thought the want of success on this occasion no great misfortune.

It was two or three o'clock on the Sunday or Monday morning when I parted from the Pretender. He acquiesced in the determination of the Regent, and declared that he would instantly set out for

Lorraine; his trunks were packed, his chaise was ordered to be at the door at five, and I sent to Paris to acquaint the Minister that he was gone. He asked me how soon I should be able to follow him, gave me commissions for some things which he desired I should bring after him, and, in a word, no Italian ever embraced the man he was going to stab with greater show of affection and confidence.

Instead of taking post for Lorraine he went to the little house in the Bois de Boulogne where his female Ministers resided; and there he continued lurking for several days, and pleasing himself with the air of mystery and business, whilst the only real business which he should have had at that time lay neglected. He saw the Spanish and Swedish Ministers in this place. I cannot tell, for I never thought it worth asking, whether he saw the Duke of Orleans; possibly he might. To have been teased into such a step, which signified nothing, and which gave the cabal an air of credit and importance, is agreeable enough to the levity of his Royal Highness's character.

The Thursday following, the Duke of Ormond came to see me, and after the compliment of telling me that he believed I should be surprised at the message he brought, he put into my hands a note to himself and a little scrip of paper directed to me, and drawn in the style of a justice of peace's warrant. They were both in the Chevalier's handwriting, and they were dated on the Tuesday, in order to make me believe that they had been written on the road and sent back to the duke; his Grace dropped in our conversation with great dexterity all the insinuations proper to confirm me in this opinion. I knew at this time his master was not gone, so that he gave me two very risible scenes, which are frequently to be met with when some people meddle in business; I mean that of seeing a man labour with a great deal of awkward artifice to make a secret of a nothing, and that of seeing yourself taken for a bubble when you know as much of the matter as he who thinks that he imposes on you.

I cannot recollect precisely the terms of the two papers. I remember that the kingly laconic style of one of them, and the expression of having no further occasion for my service, made me smile. The other was an order to give up the papers in my office, all which might have been contained in a letter-case of a moderate size. I gave the

duke the Seals and some papers which I could readily come at.
Some others - and, indeed, all such as I had not destroyed - I sent
afterwards to the Chevalier; and I took care to convey to him by a
safe hand several of his letters which it would have been very improper the duke should have seen. I am surprised that he did not
reflect on the consequence of my obeying his order literally. It depended on me to have shown his general what an opinion the
Chevalier had of his capacity. I scorned the trick, and would not
appear piqued when I was far from being angry. As I gave up without scruple all the papers which remained in my hands, because I
was determined never to make use of them, so I confess to you that
I took a sort of pride in never asking for those of mine which were
in the Pretender's hands; I contented myself with making the duke
understand how little need there was to get rid of a man in this
manner who had made the bargain which I had done at my engagement, and with taking this first opportunity to declare that I
would never more have to do with the Pretender or his cause.

That I might avoid being questioned and quoted in the most curious
and the most babbling town in the world, I related what had passed
to three or four of my friends, and hardly stirred abroad during a
fortnight out of a little lodging which very few people knew of. At
the end of this term the Marshal of Berwick came to see me, and
asked me what I meant to confine myself to my chamber when my
name was trumpeted about in all the companies of Paris, and the
most infamous stories were spread concerning me. This was the
first notice I had, and it was soon followed by others. I appeared
immediately in the world, and found there was hardly a scurrilous
tongue which had not been let loose on my subject; and that those
persons whom the Duke of Ormond and Earl of Mar must influence, or might silence, were the loudest in defaming me.

Particular instances wherein I had failed were cited; and as it was
the fashion for every Jacobite to affect being in the secret, you might
have found a multitude of vouchers to facts which, if they had been
true, could in the nature of them be known to very few persons.

This method of beating down the reputation of a man by noise and
impudence imposed on the world at first, convinced people who

were not acquainted with me, and staggered even my friends. But it ceased in a few days to have any effect against me. The malice was too gross to pass upon reflection. These stories died away almost as fast as they were published, for this very reason, because they were particular.

They gave out, for instance, that I had taken to my own use a very great sum of the Chevalier's money, when it was notorious that I had spent a great sum of my own in his service, and never would be obliged to him for a farthing, in which case, I believe, I was single. Upon this head it was easy to appeal to a very honest gentleman, the Queen's Treasurer at St. Germains, through whose hands, and not through mine, went the very little money which the Chevalier had.

They gave out that whilst he was in Scotland he never heard from me, though it was notorious that I sent him no less than five expresses during the six weeks which he consumed in this expedition. It was easy, on this head, to appeal to the persons to whom my despatches had been committed.

These lies, and many others of the same sort, which were founded on particular facts, were disproved by particular facts, and had not time - at least at Paris - to make any impression. But the principal crime with which they charged me then, and the only one which since that time they have insisted upon, is of another nature. This part of their accusation is general, and it cannot be refuted without doing what I have done above, deducing several facts, comparing these facts together, and reasoning upon them; nay, that which is worse is, that it cannot be fully refuted without the mention of some facts which, in my present circumstances, it would not be very prudent, though I should think it very lawful, for me to divulge. You see that I mean the starving the war in Scotland, which it is pretended might have been supported, and might have succeeded, too, if I had procured the succours which were asked - nay, if I had sent a little powder. This the Jacobites who affect moderation and candour shrug their shoulders at: they are sorry for it, but Lord Bolingbroke can never wash himself clean of this guilt; for these succours might have been obtained, and a proof that they might is that they

were so by others. These people leave the cause of this mismanage-
ment doubtful between my treachery and my want of capacity. The
Pretender, with all the false charity and real malice of one who sets
up for devotion, attributes all his misfortunes to my negligence.

The letters which were written by my secretary, above a year ago,
into England; the marginal notes which have been made since to the
letter from Avignon; and what is said above, have set this affair in
so clear a light, that whoever examines, with a fair intention, must
feel the truth, and be convinced by it. I cannot, however, forbear to
make some observations on the same subject here. It is even necessary that I should do so, in the design of making this discourse the
foundation of my justification to the Tories at present, and to the
whole world in time.

There is nothing which my enemies apprehend so much as my justification: and they have reason. But they may comfort themselves
with this reflection - that it will be a misfortune which will accompany me to my grave, that I suffered a chain of accidents to draw
me into such measures and such company; that I have been obliged
to defend myself against such accusations and such accusers; that
by associating with so much folly and so much knavery I am become the victim of both; that I was distressed by the former, when
the latter would have been less grievous to me, since it is much
better in business to be yoked to knaves than fools; and that I put
into their hands the means of loading me, like the scape-goat, with
all the evil consequences of their folly.

In the first letters which I received from the Earl of Mar he wrote for
arms, for ammunition, for money, for officers, and all things frankly, as if these things had been ready, and I had engaged to supply
him with them, before he set up the standard at the Brae of Mar;
whereas our condition could not be unknown to his lordship; and
you have seen that I did all I could to prevent his reckoning on any
assistance from hence. As our hopes at this Court decreased, his
lordship rose in his demands; and at the time when it was visible
that the Regent intended nothing less than even privately and indirectly to support the Scotch, the Pretender and the Earl of Mar
wrote for regular forces and a train of artillery, which was in effect

to insist that France should enter into a war for them. I might, in answer to the first instances, have asked Lord Mar what he did in Scotland, and what he meant by drawing his countrymen into a war at this time, or at least upon this foot? He who had dictated not long before a memorial wherein it was asserted that to have a prospect of succeeding in this enterprise there must be a universal insurrection, and that such an insurrection was in no sort probable, unless a body of troops was brought to support it? He who thought that the consequence of failing, when the attempt was once made, must be the utter ruin of the cause and the loss of the British liberty? He who concurred in demanding as a *pis-aller*, and the least which could be insisted on, arms, ammunition, artillery, money, and officers? I say, I might have asked what he meant to begin the dance when he had not the least assurance of any succour, but, on the contrary, the greatest reason imaginable to believe this affair was become as desperate abroad by the death of the most Christian King as it was at home by the discovery of the design and by the measures taken to defeat it?

Instead of acting this part, which would have been wise, I took that which was plausible. I resolved to contribute all I could to support the business, since it was begun. I encouraged his lordship as long as I had the least ground for doing so, and I confirmed the Pretender in his resolution of going to Scotland when he had nothing better left him to do. If I have anything to reproach myself with in the whole progress of the war in Scotland, it is having encouraged Lord Mar too long. But, on the other hand, if I had given up the cause, and had written despondingly to him before this Court had explained itself as fully as the Marshal d'Huxelles did in the conversation which is mentioned above, it is easy to see what turn would have been given to such a conduct.

The true cause of all the misfortunes which happened to the Scotch and to those who took arms in the North of England lies here - that they rose without any previous certainty of foreign help, in direct contradiction to the scheme which their leaders themselves had formed. The excuse which I have heard made for this is that the Act of Parliament for curbing the Highlanders was near to be put in execution; that they would have been disarmed, and entirely disabled from rising at any other time, if they had not rose at this. You can judge better than I of the validity of this excuse. It seems to me that by management they might have gained time, and that even when they had been reduced to the dilemma supposed, they ought to have got together under pretence of resisting the infractions of the Union without any mention of the Pretender, and have treated with the Government on this foot. By these means they might probably have preserved themselves in a condition of avowing their design when they should be sure of being backed from abroad. At the worst, they might have declared for the Chevalier when all other expedients failed them. In a word, I take this excuse not to be very good, and the true reason of this conduct to have been the rashness of the people and the inconsistent measures of their head.

But admitting the excuse to be valid, it remains still an undeniable truth that this is the original fountain from whence all those waters of bitterness flowed which so many unhappy people have drunk of. I have said already that the necessity of acting was precipitated before any measures to act with success had been taken, and that the necessity of doing so seemed to increase as the means of doing so were taken away. To whom is this to be ascribed? Is it to be ascribed to me, who had no share in these affairs till a few weeks before the Duke of Ormond was forced to abandon England, and the discovery of the intended invasion was published to Parliament and to the world? or is it to be ascribed to those who had from the first been at the head of this undertaking?

Unable to defend this point, the next resort of the Jacobites is to this impudent and absurd affirmation - that, notwithstanding the disadvantages under which they took arms, they should have succeeded if the indirect assistances which were asked from France had been obtained. Nay, that they should have been able to defend the Highlands if I had sent them a little powder. Is it possible that a man should be wounded with such blunt weapons? Much more than powder was asked for from the first, and I have already said that when the Chevalier came into Scotland, regular troops, artillery, etc., were demanded. Both he and the Earl of Mar judged it impossible to stand their ground without such assistance as these. How scandalous, then, must it be deemed that they suffer their dependents to spread in the world that for want of a little powder I forced them to abandon Scotland! The Earl of Mar knows that all the powder in France would not have enabled him to stay at Perth as long as he did if he had not had another security. And when that failed him, he must have quitted the party, if the Regent had given us all that he made some of us expect.

But to finish all that I intend to say on a subject which has tired me, and perhaps you; the Jacobites affirm that the indirect assistances which they desired, might have been obtained; and I confess that I am inexcusable if this fact be true. To prove it, they appeal to the little politicians of whom I have spoken so often. I affirm, on the contrary, that nothing could be obtained here to support the Scotch or to encourage the English. To prove the assertion, I appeal to the Ministers with whom I negotiated, and to the Regent himself, who, whatever language he may hold in private with other people, cannot controvert with me the truth of what I advance. He excluded me formerly, that he might the more easily avoid doing anything; and perhaps he has blamed me since, that he might excuse his doing nothing. All this may be true, and yet it will remain true that he would never have been prevailed upon to act directly against his interest in the only point of view which he has - I mean, the crown of France - and against the unanimous sense of all his Ministers. Suppose that in the time of the late Queen, when she had the peace in view, a party in France had implored her assistance, and had applied to Margery Fielding, to Israel, to my Lady Oglethorpe, to Dr. Battle, and Lieutenant-General Stewart, what success do you imagine such applications would have had? The Queen would have spoke them fair - she would speak otherwise to nobody; but do you imagine she would have made one step in their favour? Olive Trant, Magny, Mademoiselle Chaussery, a dirty Abbi Brigault, and Mr. Dillon, are characters very apposite to these. And what I suppose to have passed in England is not a whit more ridiculous than what really passed here.

I say nothing of the ships which the Jacobites pretend that they sent into Scotland three weeks or a month after the Pretender was returned. I believe they might have had my Lord Stair's connivance then, as well as the Regent's. I say nothing of the order which they

pretend to have obtained, and which I never saw, for the stores that
were seized at Havre to be delivered to Castel Blanco. I have already said enough on this head, and you cannot have failed to observe that this signal favour was never obtained by these people till
the Marshal d'Huxelles had owned to me that nothing was to be
expected from France, and that the only thing which I could do was
to endeavour to bring the Pretender, the Earl of Mar, and the principal persons who were most exposed, off, neither he nor I imagining that any such would be left behind.

When I began to appear in the world, upon the advertisements
which my friends gave me of the clamour that was raised against
me, you will easily think I did not enter into so many particulars as I
have done with you. I said even less than you have seen in those
letters which Brinsden wrote into England in March and April was
twelvemonth, and yet the clamour sank immediately. The people of
consideration at this Court beat it down, and the Court of St. Germains grew so ashamed of it that the Queen thought fit to purge
herself of having had any share in encouraging the discourses
which were held against me, or having been so much as let into the
secret of the measure which preceded them. The provocation was
great, but I resolved to act without passion. I saw the advantage the
Pretender and his council, who disposed of things better for me
than I should have done for myself, had given me; but I saw likewise that I must improve this advantage with the utmost caution.

As I never imagined that he would treat me in the manner he did,
nor that his Ministers could be weak enough to advise him to it, I
had resolved, on his return from Scotland, to follow him till his
residence should be fixed somewhere or other. After which, having
served the Tories in this which I looked upon as their last struggle
for power, and having continued to act in the Pretender's affairs till
the end of the term for which I embarked with him, I should have
esteemed myself to be at liberty, and should in the civillest manner I
was able have taken my leave of him. Had we parted thus, I should
have remained in a very strange situation during the rest of my life;
but I had examined myself thoroughly, I was determined, I was
prepared.

On one side he would have thought that he had a sort of right on any future occasion to call me out of my retreat; the Tories would probably have thought the same thing: my resolution was taken to refuse them both, and I foresaw that both would condemn me. On the other side, the consideration of his keeping measures with me, joined to that of having once openly declared for him, would have created a point of honour by which I should have been tied down, not only from ever engaging against him, but also from making my peace at home. The Chevalier cut this gordian knot asunder at one blow. He broke the links of that chain which former engagements had fastened on me, and gave me a right to esteem myself as free from all obligations of keeping measures with him as I should have continued if I had never engaged in his interest. I took therefore, from that moment, the resolution of making my peace at home, and of employing all the unfortunate experience I had acquired abroad to undeceive my friends and to promote the union and the quiet of my country.

The Earl of Stair had received a full power to treat with me whilst I was engaged with the Pretender, as I have been since informed. He had done me the justice to believe me incapable to hearken, in such circumstances, to any proposals of that kind; and as much friend-ship as he had for me, as much as I had for him, we entertained not the least even indirect correspondence together during that whole time. Soon afterwards he employed a person to communicate to me the disposition of his Majesty to grant me my pardon, and his own desire to give me, on this occasion, all the proofs he could of his inclination in my favour. I embraced the offer, as it became me to do, with all possible sense of the King's goodness, and of his lord-ship's friendship. We met, we talked together, and he wrote to the Court on the subject. The turn which the Ministers gave to this mat-ter was, to enter into a treaty to reverse my attainder, and to stipu-late the conditions on which this act of grace should be granted me.

The notion of a treaty shocked me. I resolved never to be restored rather than go that way to work; and I opened myself without any reserve to Lord Stair. I told him that I looked on myself to be obliged in honour and in conscience to undeceive my friends in England, both as to the state of foreign affairs, as to the management of the Jacobite interest abroad, and as to the characters of persons - in every one of which points I knew them to be most grossly and most dangerously deluded; that the treatment I had received from the Pretender and his adherents would justify me to the world in doing this; that if I remained in exile all my life, he might be assured that I would never more have to do with the Jacobite cause; and that if I was restored, I should give it an effectual blow, in making that apology which the Pretender has put me under a necessity of making: that in doing this I flattered myself that I should contribute something to the establishment of the King's Government, and to the union of his subjects; but that this was all the merit which I could promise to have; that if the Court believed these professions to be sincere, a treaty with me was unnecessary for them; and that if they did not believe them so, a treaty with them was dangerous for me; that I was determined in this whole transaction to make no one step which I would not own in the face of the world; that in other circumstances it might be sufficient to act honestly, but that in a case as extraordinary as mine it was necessary to act clearly, and to leave no room for the least doubtful construction.

The Earl of Stair, as well as Mr. Craggs, who arrived soon after in France, came into my sense. I have reason to believe that the King has approved it likewise upon their representations, since he has been pleased to give me the most gracious assurances of his favour. What the effect of all this may be in the next or in any other Session, I know not; but this is the foot on which I have put myself, and on which I stand at the moment I write to you. The Whigs may continue inveterate, and by consequence frustrate his Majesty's good intentions towards me; the Tories may continue to rail at me, on the credit of such enemies as I have described to you in the course of this relation: neither the one nor the other shall make me swerve out of the path which I have traced to myself.

I have now led you through the several stages which I proposed at first; and I should do wrong to your good understanding, as well as to our mutual friendship, if I suspected that you could hold any other language to me than that which Dolabella uses to Cicero: "Satisfactum est jam a te vel officio vel familiaritati; satisfactum etiam partibus." The King, who pardons me, might complain of me; the

Whigs might declaim against me; my family might reproach me for the little regard which I have shown to my own and to their interests; but where is the crime I have been guilty of towards my party and towards my friends? In what part of my conduct will the Tories find an excuse for the treatment which they have given me? As Tories such as they were when I left England, I defy them to find any. But here lies the sore, and, tender as it is, I must lay it open. Those amongst them who rail at me now are changed from what they were, or from what they professed themselves to be, when we lived and acted together. They were Tories then; they are Jacobites now. Their objections to the course of my conduct whilst I was in the Pretender's interest are the pretence; the true reason of their anger is, that I renounce the Pretender for my life. When you were first driven into this interest, I may appeal to you for the notion which the party had. You thought of restoring him by the strength of the Tories, and of opposing a Tory king to a Whig king. You took him up as the instrument of your revenge and of your ambition. You looked on him as your creature, and never once doubted of making what terms you pleased with him. This is so true that the same language is still held to the catechumens in Jacobitism. Were the contrary to be avowed even now, the party in England would soon diminish. I engaged on this principle when your orders sent me to Commercy, and I never acted on any other. This ought to have been part of my merit towards the Tories; and it would have been so if they had continued in the same dispositions. But they are changed, and this very thing is become my crime. Instead of making the Pretender their tool, they are his. Instead of having in view to restore him on their own terms, they are labouring to do it without any terms; that is, to speak properly, they are ready to receive him on his. Be not deceived: there is not a man on this side of the water who acts in any other manner. The Church of England Jacobite and the Irish Papist seem in every respect to have the same cause. Those on your side of the water who correspond with these are to be comprehended in the same class; and from hence it is that the clamour raised against me has been kept up with so much industry, and is redoubled on the least appearance of my return home, and of my being in a situation to justify myself.

You have seen already what reasons the Pretender, and the several sorts of people who compose his party here, had to get rid of me, and to cover me to the utmost of their power with infamy. Their views were as short in this case as they are in all others. They did not see at first that this conduct would not only give me a right, but put me under a necessity of keeping no farther measures with them, and of laying the whole mystery of their iniquity open. As soon as they discovered this, they took the only course which was left them - that of poisoning the minds of the Tories, and of creating such prejudices against me whilst I remained in a condition of not speaking for myself, as will they hope prevent the effect of whatever I may say when I am in a condition of pleading my own cause. The bare apprehension that I shall show the world that I have been guilty of no crime renders me criminal among these men; and they hold themselves ready, being unable to reply either in point of fact or in point of reason, to drown my voice in the confusion of their clamour.

The only crimes I am guilty of, I own. I own the crime of having been for the Pretender in a very different manner from those with whom I acted. I served him as faithfully, I served him as well as they; but I served him on a different principle. I own the crime of having renounced him, and of being resolved never to have to do with him as long as I live. I own the crime of being determined sooner or later, as soon as I can, to clear myself of all the unjust aspersions which have been cast upon me; to undeceive by my experience as many as I can of those Tories who may have been drawn into error; and to contribute, if ever I return home, as far as I am able, to promote the national good of Britain without any other regard. These crimes do not, I hope, by this time appear to you to be of a very black dye. You may come, perhaps, to think them virtues, when you have read and considered what remains to be said; for before I conclude, it is necessary that I open one matter to you which I could not weave in sooner without breaking too much the thread of my narration. In this place, unmingled with anything else, it will have, as it deserves to have, your whole attention.

Whoever composed that curious piece of false fact, false argument, false English, and false eloquence, the letter from Avignon, says that I was not thought the most proper person to speak about religion. I

confess I should be of his mind, and should include his patrons in
my case, if the practice of it was to be recommended; for surely it is
unpardonable impudence to impose by precept what we do not
teach by example. I should be of the same mind, if the nature of
religion was to be explained, if its mysteries were to be fathomed,
and if this great truth was to be established - that the Church of
England has the advantage over all other Churches in purity of
doctrine, and in wisdom of discipline. But nothing of this kind was
necessary. This would have been the task of reverend and learned
divines. We of the laity had nothing more to do than to lay in our
claim that we could never submit to be governed by a Prince who
was not of the religion of our country. Such a declaration could
hardly have failed of some effect towards opening the eyes and
disposing the mind even of the Pretender. At least, in justice to ourselves, and in justice to our party, we who were here ought to have
made it; and the influence of it on the Pretender ought to have become the rule of our subsequent conduct.

In thinking in this manner I think no otherwise now than I have
always thought; and I cannot forget, nor you neither, what passed
when, a little before the death of the Queen, letters were conveyed
from the Chevalier to several persons - to myself among others. In
the letter to me the article of religion was so awkwardly handled
that he made the principal motive of the confidence we ought to
have in him to consist in his firm resolution to adhere to Popery.
The effect which this epistle had on me was the same which it had
on those Tories to whom I communicated it at that time; it made us
resolve to have nothing to do with him.

Some time after this I was assured by several, and I make no doubt
but others have been so too, that the Chevalier at the bottom was
not a bigot; that whilst he remained abroad and could expect no
succour, either present or future, from any Princes but those of the
Roman Catholic Communion, it was prudent, whatever he might
think, to make no demonstration of a design to change; but that his
temper was such, and he was already so disposed, that we might
depend on his compliance with what should be desired of him if
ever he came amongst us, and was taken from under the wing of
the Queen his mother. To strengthen this opinion of his character, it

was said that he had sent for Mr. Leslie over; that he allowed him to celebrate the Church of England service in his family; and that he had promised to hear what this divine should represent on the subject of religion to him. When I came abroad, the same things, and much more, were at first insinuated to me; and I began to let them make impression upon me, notwithstanding what I had seen under his hand. I would willingly flatter myself that this impression disposed me to incline to Jacobitism rather than allow that the inclination to Jacobitism disposed me easily to believe what, upon that principle, I had so much reason to wish might be true. Which was the cause, and which the effect, I cannot well determine: perhaps they did mutually occasion each other. Thus much is certain - that I was far from weighing this matter as I ought to have done when the solicitation of my friends and the persecution of my enemies precipitated me into engagements with the Pretender.

I was willing to take it for granted that since you were as ready to declare as I believed you at that time, you must have had entire satisfaction on the article of religion. I was soon undeceived; this string had never been touched. My own observation, and the unanimous report of all those who from his infancy have approached the Pretender's person, soon taught me how difficult it is to come to terms with him on this head, and how unsafe to embark without them.

His religion is not founded on the love of virtue and the detestation of vice; on a sense of that obedience which is due to the will of the Supreme Being, and a sense of those obligations which creatures formed to live in a mutual dependence on one another lie under. The spring of his whole conduct is fear. Fear of the horns of the devil and of the flames of hell. He has been taught to believe that nothing but a blind submission to the Church of Rome and a strict adherence to all the terms of that communion can save him from these dangers. He has all the superstition of a Capuchin, but I found on him no tincture of the religion of a prince. Do not imagine that I loose the reins to my imagination, or that I write what my resentments dictate: I tell you simply my opinion. I have heard the same description of his character made by those who know him best, and I conversed with very few among the Roman Catholics themselves who did not think him too much a Papist.

Nothing gave me from the beginning so much uneasiness as the consideration of this part of his character, and of the little care which had been taken to correct it. A true turn had not been given to the first steps which were made with him. The Tories who engaged afterwards, threw themselves, as it were, at his head. He had been suffered to think that the party in England wanted him as much as he wanted them. There was no room to hope for much compliance on the head of religion when he was in these sentiments, and when he thought the Tories too far advanced to have it in their power to retreat; and little dependence was at any time to be placed on the promises of a man capable of thinking his damnation attached to the observance, and his salvation to the breach, of these very promises. Something, however, was to be done, and I thought that the least which could be done was to deal plainly with him, and to show him the impossibility of governing our nation by any other expedient than by complying with that which would be expected from him as to his religion. This was thought too much by the Duke of Ormond and Mr. Leslie; although the duke could be no more ignorant than the minister how ill the latter had been used, how far the Chevalier had been from keeping the word which he had given, and on the faith of which Mr. Leslie had come over to him. They both knew that he not only refused to hear himself, but that he sheltered the ignorance of his priests, or the badness of his cause, or both, behind his authority, and absolutely forbade all discourse concerning religion. The duke seemed convinced that it would be time enough to talk of religion to him when he should be restored, or, at soonest, when he should be landed in England; that the influence under which he had lived being at a distance, the reasonableness of what we might propose, joined to the apparent necessity which would then stare him in the face, could not fail to produce all the effects which we could desire.

To me this whole reasoning appeared fallacious. Our business was not to make him change appearances on this side of the water, but to prepare him to give those which would be necessary on the other; and there was no room to hope that if we could gain nothing on his prejudices here, we should be able to overcome them in Britain. I

would have argued just as the Duke of Ormond and Leslie if I had
been a Papist; and I saw well enough that some people about him,
for in a great dearth of ability there was cunning to be met with,
affected nothing more than to keep off all discourse of religion. To
my apprehension it was exceeding plain that we should find, if we
were once in England, the necessity of going forward at any rate
with him much greater than he would find that of complying with
us. I thought it an unpardonable fault to have taken a formal engagement with him, when no previous satisfaction had been obtained on a point at least as essential to our civil as to our religious
rights; to the peace of the State as to the prosperity of the Church;
and I looked on this fault to be aggravated by every day's delay.
Our silence was unfair both to the Chevalier and to our friends in
England. He was induced by it to believe that they would exact far
less from him than we knew they expected, and they were confirmed in an opinion of his docility, which we knew to be void of all
foundation. The pretence of removing that influence under which
he had lived was frivolous, and should never have been urged to
me, who saw plainly that, according to the measures pursued by the
very persons who urged it, he must be environed in England by the
same people that surrounded him here; and that the Court of St.
James's would be constituted, if ever he was restored, in the same
manner as that of St. Germains was.

When the draft of a declaration and other papers which were to be
dispersed in Great Britain came to be settled, it appeared that my
apprehension and distrust were but too well founded. The Pretender took exception against several passages, and particularly against
those wherein a direct promise of securing the Churches of England
and Ireland was made. He was told, he said, that he could not in
conscience make such a promise, and, the debate being kept up a
little while, he asked me with some warmth why the Tories were so
desirous to have him if they expected those things from him which
his religion did not allow. I left these drafts, by his order, with him,
that he might consider and amend them. I cannot say that he sent
them to the Queen to be corrected by her confessor and the rest of
her council, but I firmly believe it. Sure I am that he took time sufficient to do this before he sent them from Bar, where he then was, to
Paris, whither I was returned. When they were digested in such a

manner as satisfied his casuists he made them be printed, and my
name was put to the declaration, as if the original had been signed
by me. I had hitherto submitted my opinion to the judgment of
others, but on this occasion I took advice from myself. I declared to
him that I would not suffer my name to be at the bottom of this
paper. All the copies which came to my hands I burnt, and another
was printed off without any countersigning.

The whole tenor of the amendments was one continued instance of
the grossest bigotry, and the most material passages were turned
with all the Jesuitical prevarication imaginable. As much as it was
his interest at that time to cultivate the respect which many of the
Tories really had for the memory of the late Queen, and which
many others affected as a farther mark of their opposition to the
Court and to the Whig party; as much as it was his interest to weave
the honour of her name into his cause, and to render her, even after
her death, a party to the dispute, he could not be prevailed upon to
give her that character which her enemies allowed her, nor to make
use of those expressions, in speaking of her, which, by the general
manner of their application, are come to be little more than terms of
respect and words of form proper in the style of public acts. For
instance:-

She was called in the original draft "his sister of glorious and
blessed memory." In that which he published, the epithet of
"blessed" was left out. Her eminent justice and her exemplary piety
were occasionally mentioned; in lieu of which he substituted a flat,
and, in this case, an invidious expression, "her inclinations to justice."

Not content with declaring her neither just nor pious in this world
he did little less than declare her damned in the other, according to
the charitable principles of the Church of Rome.

"When it pleased Almighty God to take her to Himself," was the
expression used in speaking of the death of the Queen. This he
erased, and instead thereof inserted these words: "When it pleased
Almighty God to put a period to her life."

He graciously allowed the Universities to be nurseries of loyalty;
but did not think that it became him to style them "nurseries of
religion."

Since his father passes already for a saint, and since reports are encouraged of miracles which they suppose to be wrought at his
tomb, he might have allowed his grandfather to pass for a martyr;
but he struck out of the draft these words, "that blessed martyr who
died for his people," which were applied to King Charles I., and
would say nothing more of him than that "he fell a sacrifice to rebellion."

In the clause which related to the Churches of England and Ireland
there was a plain and direct promise inserted of "effectual provision
for their security, and for their re-establishment in all those rights
which belong to them." This clause was not suffered to stand, but
another was formed, wherein all mention of the Church of Ireland
was omitted, and nothing was promised to the Church of England
but the security, and "re-establishment of all those rights, privileges,
immunities, and possessions which belong to her," and wherein he
had already promised by his declaration of the 20th of July, to secure and "protect all her members."

I need make no comment on a proceeding so easy to be understood.
The drift of these evasions, and of this affected obscurity, is obvious
enough - at least, it will appear so by the observations which remain
to be made.

He was so afraid of admitting any words which might be construed
into a promise of his consenting to those things which should be
found necessary for the present or future security of our constitution, that in a paragraph where he was made to say that he thought
himself obliged to be solicitous for the prosperity of the Church of
England, the word prosperity was expunged, and we were left by
this mental reservation to guess what he was solicitous for. It could
not be for her prosperity: that he had expunged. It must therefore be
for her destruction, which in his language would have been styled
her conversion.

Another remarkable proof of the same kind is to be found towards the conclusion of the declaration. After having spoken of the peace and flourishing estate of the kingdom, he was made to express his readiness to concert with the two Houses such further measures as should be thought necessary for securing the same to future generations. The design of this paragraph you see. He and his council saw it too, and therefore the word "securing" was laid aside, and the word "leaving" was inserted in lieu of it.

One would imagine that a declaration corrected in this manner might have been suffered to go abroad without any farther precaution. But these papers had been penned by Protestants; and who could answer that there might not be still ground sufficient from the tenor of them to insist on everything necessary for the security of that religion? The declaration of the 20th of July had been penned by a priest of the Scotch college, and the expressions had been measured so as to suit perfectly with the conduct which the Chevalier intended to hold; so as to leave room to distinguish him, upon future occasions, with the help of a little pious sophistry, out of all the engagements which he seemed to take in it. This orthodox paper was therefore to accompany the heretical paper into the world, and no promise of moment was to stand in the latter, unless qualified by a reference to the former. Thus the Church was to be secured in the rights, etc., which belong to her. How? No otherwise than according to the declaration of the month of July. And what does that promise? Security and protection to the members of this Church in the enjoyment of their property. I make no doubt but Bellarmine, if he had been the Chevalier's confessor, would have passed this paragraph thus amended. No engagement whatever taken in favour of the Church of Ireland, and a happy distinction found between securing that of England, and protecting her members. Many a useful project for the destruction of heretics, and for accumulating power and riches to the See of Rome, has been established on a more slender foundation.

The same spirit reigns through the whole. Civil and religious rights are no otherwise to be confirmed than in conformity to the declaration of July; nay, the general pardon is restrained and limited to the terms prescribed therein.

This is the account which I judged too important to be omitted, and which I chose to give you all together. I shall surely be justified at present in concluding that the Tories are grossly deluded in their opinion of this Prince's character, or else that they sacrifice all which ought to be esteemed precious and sacred among men to their passions. In both these cases I remain still a Tory, and am true to the party. In the first, I endeavour to undeceive you by an experience purchased at my expense and for your sakes: in the second, I endeavour to prevail on you to revert to that principle from which we have deviated. You never intended, whilst I lived amongst you, the ruin of your country; and yet every step which you now make towards the restoration you are so fond of, is a step towards this ruin. No man of sense, well informed, can ever go into measures for it, unless he thinks himself and his country in such desperate circumstances that nothing is left them but to choose of two ruins that which they like best.

The exile of the royal family, under Cromwell's usurpation, was the principal cause of all those misfortunes in which Britain has been involved, as well as of many of those which have happened to the rest of Europe, during more than half a century.

The two brothers, Charles and James, became then infected with Popery to such degrees as their different characters admitted of. Charles had parts, and his good understanding served as an antidote to repel the poison. James, the simplest man of his time, drank off the whole chalice. The poison met in his composition with all the fear, all the credulity, and all the obstinacy of temper proper to increase its virulence and to strengthen its effect. The first had always a wrong bias upon him; he connived at the establishment, and indirectly contributed to the growth, of that power which afterwards disturbed the peace and threatened the liberty of Europe so often; but he went no further out of the way. The opposition of his Parliaments and his own reflections stopped him here. The Prince and the people were, indeed, mutually jealous of one another, from whence much present disorder flowed, and the foundation of future evils was laid; but his good and his bad principles combating still together, he maintained, during a reign of more than twenty years, in some tolerable degree, the authority of the Crown and the flourishing estate of the nation. The last, drunk with superstitious and even enthusiastic zeal, ran headlong into his own ruin whilst he endeavoured to precipitate ours. His Parliament and his people did all they could to save themselves by winning him. But all was vain; he had no principle on which they could take hold. Even his good qualities worked against them, and his love of his country went halves with his bigotry. How he succeeded we have heard from our fathers. The revolution of 1688 saved the nation and ruined the King.

Now the Pretender's education has rendered him infinitely less fit than his uncle - and at least as unfit as his father - to be King of Great Britain. Add to this that there is no resource in his understanding. Men of the best sense find it hard to overcome religious prejudices, which are of all the strongest; but he is a slave to the weakest. The rod hangs like the sword of Damocles over his head, and he trembles before his mother and his priest. What, in the name of God, can any member of the Church of England promise himself from such a character? Are we by another revolution to return into the same state from which we were delivered by the first? Let us take example from the Roman Catholics, who act very reasonably in refusing to submit to a Protestant Prince. Henry IV. had at least as good a title to the crown of France as the Pretender has to ours. His religion alone stood in his way, and he had never been King if he had not removed that obstacle. Shall we submit to a Popish Prince, who will no more imitate Henry IV. in changing his religion than he will imitate those shining qualities which rendered him the honestest gentleman, the bravest captain, and the greatest prince of his age? Allow me to give a loose to my pen for a moment on this subject. General benevolence and universal charity seem to be established in the Gospel as the distinguishing badges of Christianity. How it happens I cannot tell; but so it is, that in all ages of the Church the professors of Christianity seem to have been animated by a quite contrary spirit. Whilst they were thinly scattered over the world, tolerated in some places, but established nowhere, their zeal often consumed their charity. Paganism, at that time the religion by law established, was insulted by many of them; the ceremonies were disturbed, the altars thrown down. As soon as, by the favour of Constantine, their numbers were increased, and the reins of government were put into their hands, they began to employ the secular arm, not only against different religions, but against different sects which arose in their own religion. A man may boldly affirm that more blood has been shed in the disputes between Christian and Christian than has ever been drawn from the whole body of them in the persecutions of the heathen emperors and in the conquests of the Mahometan princes. From these they have received quarter, but never from one another. The Christian religion is actually tolerated among the Mahometans, and the domes of churches and mosques arise in the same city. But it will be hard to find an example where one sect of Christians has tolerated another which it was in their power to extirpate. They have gone farther in these later ages; what was practised formerly has been taught since. Persecution has been reduced into system, and the disciples of the meek and humble Jesus have avowed a tyranny which the most barbarous conquerors never claimed. The wicked subtilty of casuists has established breach of faith with those who differ from us as a duty in opposition to faith, and murder itself has been made one of the means of salvation. I know very well that the Reformed Churches have been far from going those cruel lengths which are authorised by the doctrine as well as example of that of Rome, though Calvin put a flaming sword on the title of a French edition of his Institute, with this motto, "Je ne suis point venu mettre la paix, mais l'epie;" but I know likewise that the difference lies in the means and not in the aim of their policy. The Church of England, the most humane of all of them, would root out every other religion if it was in her power. She would not hang and burn; her measures would be milder, and therefore, perhaps, more effectual.

Since, then, there is this inveterate rancour among Christians, can anything be more absurd than for those of one persuasion to trust the supreme power, or any part of it, to those of another? Particularly must it not be reputed madness in those of our religion to trust themselves in the hands of Roman Catholics? Must it not be reputed impudence in a Roman Catholic to expect that we should? he who looks upon us as heretics, as men in rebellion against a lawful - nay, a divine - authority, and whom it is, therefore, meritorious by all sorts of ways to reduce to obedience? There are many, I know, amongst them who think more generously, and whose morals are not corrupted by that which is called religion; but this is the spirit of the priesthood, in whose scale that scrap of a parable, "Compel them to come in," which they apply as they please, outweighs the whole Decalogue. This will be the spirit of every man who is bigot enough to be under their direction; and so much is sufficient for my present purpose.

During your last Session of Parliament it was expected that the Whigs would attempt to repeal the Occasional Bill. The same jealousy continues; there is, perhaps, foundation for it. Give me leave to ask you upon what principle we argued for making this law, and upon what principle you must argue against the repeal of it. I have mentioned the principle in the beginning of this discourse. No man ought to be trusted with any share of power under a Government who must, to act consistently with himself, endeavour the destruction of that very Government. Shall this proposition pass for true when it is applied to keep a Presbyterian from being mayor of a corporation, and shall it become false when it is applied to keep a Papist from being king? The proposition is equally true in both cases; but the argument drawn from it is just so much stronger in the latter than in the former case, as the mischiefs which may result from the power and influence of a king are greater than those which can be wrought by a magistrate of the lowest order. This seems to my apprehension to be *argumentum ad hominem,* and I do not see by what happy distinction a Jacobite Tory could elude the force of it.

It may be said, and it has been urged to me, that if the Chevalier was restored, the knowledge of his character would be our security; "habet fœnum in cornu;" there would be no pretence for trusting him, and by consequence it would be easy to put such restrictions on the exercise of the regal power as might hinder him from invading or sapping our religion and liberty. But this I utterly deny. Experience has shown us how ready men are to court power and profit, and who can determine how far either the Tories or the Whigs would comply, in order to secure to themselves the enjoyment of all the places in the kingdom? Suppose, however, that a majority of true Israelites should be found, whom no temptation could oblige to bow the knee to Baal; in order to preserve the Government on one hand must they not destroy it on the other? The necessary restrictions would in this case be so many and so important as to leave hardly the shadow of a monarchy if he submitted to them; and if he did not submit to them, these patriots would have no resource left but in rebellion. Thus, therefore, the affair would turn if the Pretender was restored. We might, most probably, lose our religion and liberty by the bigotry of the Prince and the corruption of the people. We should have no chance of preserving them but by an entire change of the whole frame of our Government or by another revolution. What reasonable man would voluntarily reduce himself to the necessity of making an option among such melancholy alternatives?

The best which could be hoped for, were the Chevalier on the throne, would be that a thread of favourable accidents, improved by the wisdom and virtue of Parliament, might keep off the evil day during his reign. But still the fatal cause would be established; it would be entailed upon us, and every man would be apprised that sooner or later the fatal effect must follow. Consider a little what a condition we should be in, both with respect to our foreign interest and our domestic quiet, whilst the reprieve lasted, whilst the Chevalier or his successors made no direct attack upon the constitution.

As to the first, it is true, indeed, that princes and States are friends or foes to one another according as the motives of ambition drive them. These are the first principles of union and division amongst them. The Protestant Powers of Europe have joined, in our days, to support and aggrandise the House of Austria, as they did in the days of our forefathers to defeat her designs and to reduce her power; and the most Christian King of France has more than once joined his councils, and his arms too, with the councils and arms of the most Mahometan Emperor of Constantinople. But still there is, and there must continue, as long as the influence of the Papal authority subsists in Europe, another general, permanent, and invariable division of interests. The powers of earth, like those of heaven, have two distinct motions. Each of them rolls in his own political orb, but each of them is hurried at the same time round the great vortex of his religion. If this general notion be just, apply it to the present case. Whilst a Roman Catholic holds the rudder, how can we expect to be steered in our proper course? His political interest will certainly incline him to direct our first motion right, but his mistaken religious interest will render him incapable of doing it steadily.

As to the last, our domestic quiet; even whilst the Chevalier and those of his race concealed their game, we should remain in the most unhappy state which human nature is subject to, a state of doubt and suspense. Our preservation would depend on making him the object of our eternal jealousy, who, to render himself and his people happy, ought to be that of our entire confidence.

Whilst the Pretender and his successors forbore to attack the religion and liberty of the nation, we should remain in the condition of those people who labour under a broken constitution, or who carry about them some chronical distemper. They feel a little pain at every moment; or a certain uneasiness, which is sometimes less tolerable than pain, hangs continually on them, and they languish in the constant expectation of dying perhaps in the severest torture.

But if the fear of hell should dissipate all other fears in the Pretender's mind, and carry him, which is frequently the effect of that passion, to the most desperate undertakings; if among his successors a man bold enough to make the attempt should arise, the condition of the British nation would be still more deplorable. The attempt succeeding, we should fall into tyranny; for a change of religion could never be brought about by consent; and the same force that would be sufficient to enslave our consciences, would be sufficient for all the other purposes of arbitrary power. The attempt failing, we should fall into anarchy; for there is no medium when disputes between a prince and his people are arrived at a certain point; he must either be submitted to or deposed.

I have now laid before you even more than I intended to have said when I took my pen, and I am persuaded that if these papers ever come to your hands, they will enable you to cast up the account between party and me. Till the time of the Queen's death it stands, I believe, even between us. The Tories distinguished me by their approbation and by the credit which I had amongst them, and I endeavoured to distinguish myself in their service, under the immediate weight of great discouragement and with the not very distant prospect of great danger. Since that time the account is not so even, and I dare appeal to any impartial person whether my side in it be that of the debtor. As to the opinion of mankind in general, and the judgment which posterity will pass on these matters, I am under no great concern. "Suum cuique decus posteritas rependit."

A LETTER TO ALEXANDER POPE

Dear Sir, - Since you have begun, at my request, the work which I have wished long that you would undertake, it is but reasonable that I submit to the task you impose upon me. The mere compliance with anything you desire, is a pleasure to me. On the present occasion, however, this compliance is a little interested; and that I may not assume more merit with you than I really have, I will own that in performing this act of friendship - for such you are willing to esteem it - the purity of my motive is corrupted by some regard to my private utility. In short, I suspect you to be guilty of a very friendly fraud, and to mean my service whilst you seem to mean your own.

In leading me to discourse, as you have done often, and in pressing me to write, as you do now, on certain subjects, you may propose to draw me back to those trains of thought which are, above all others, worthy to employ the human mind: and I thank you for it. They have been often interrupted by the business and dissipations of the world, but they were never so more grievously to me, nor less usefully to the public, than since royal seduction prevailed on me to abandon the quiet and leisure of the retreat I had chosen abroad, and to neglect the example of Rutilius, for I might have imitated him in this at least, who fled further from his country when he was invited home.

You have begun your ethic epistles in a masterly manner. You have copied no other writer, nor will you, I think, be copied by any one.

It is with genius as it is with beauty; there are a thousand pretty things that charm alike; but superior genius, like superior beauty, has always something particular, something that belongs to itself alone. It is always distinguishable, not only from those who have no claim to excellence, but even from those who excel, when any such there are.

I am pleased, you may be sure, to find your satire turn, in the very beginning of these epistles, against the principal cause - for such you know that I think it - of all the errors, all the contradictions, and all the disputes which have arisen among those who impose them-selves on their fellow-creatures for great masters, and almost sole proprietors of a gift of God which is common to the whole species. This gift is reason; a faculty, or rather an aggregate of faculties, that is bestowed in different degrees; and not in the highest, certainly, on those who make the highest pretensions to it. Let your satire chastise, and, if it be possible, humble that pride, which is the fruit-ful parent of their vain curiosity and bold presumption; which ren-ders them dogmatical in the midst of ignorance, and often sceptical in the midst of knowledge. The man who is puffed up with this philosophical pride, whether divine or theist, or atheist, deserves no more to be respected than one of those trifling creatures who are conscious of little else than their animality, and who stop as far short of the attainable perfections of their nature as the other at-tempts to go beyond them. You will discover as many silly affec-tions, as much foppery and futility, as much inconsistency and low artifice in one as in the other. I never met the mad woman at Brent-ford decked out in old and new rags, and nice and fantastical in the manner of wearing them, without reflecting on many of the pro-found scholars and sublime philosophers of our own and of former ages.

You may expect some contradiction and some obloquy on the part of these men, though you will have less to apprehend from their malice and resentment than a writer in prose on the same subjects would have. You will be safer in the generalities of poetry; and I know your precaution enough to know that you will screen yourself in them against any direct charge of heterodoxy. But the great cla-mour of all will be raised when you descend lower, and let your

Muse loose among the herd of mankind. Then will those powers of dulness whom you have ridiculed into immortality be called forth in one united phalanx against you. But why do I talk of what may happen? You have experienced lately something more than I prognosticate. Fools and knaves should be modest at least; they should ask quarter of men of sense and virtue: and so they do till they grow up to a majority, till a similitude of character assures them of the protection of the great. But then vice and folly such as prevail in our country, corrupt our manners, deform even social life, and contribute to make us ridiculous as well as miserable, will claim respect for the sake of the vicious and the foolish. It will be then no longer sufficient to spare persons; for to draw even characters of imagination must become criminal when the application of them to those of highest rank and greatest power cannot fail to be made. You began to laugh at the ridiculous taste or the no taste in gardening and building of some men who are at great expense in both. What a clamour was raised instantly! The name of Timon was applied to a noble person with double malice, to make him ridiculous, and you, who lived in friendship with him, odious. By the authority that employed itself to encourage this clamour, and by the industry used to spread and support it, one would have thought that you had directed your satire in that epistle to political subjects, and had inveighed against those who impoverish, dishonour, and sell their country, instead of making yourself inoffensively merry at the expense of men who ruin none but themselves, and render none but themselves ridiculous. What will the clamour be, and how will the same authority foment it, when you proceed to lash, in other instances, our want of elegance even in luxury, and our wild profusion, the source of insatiable rapacity, and almost universal venality? My mind forebodes that the time will come - and who knows how near it may be? - when other powers than those of Grub Street may be drawn forth against you, and when vice and folly may be avowedly sheltered behind a power instituted for better and contrary purposes - for the punishment of one, and for the reformation of both.

But, however this may be, pursue your task undauntedly, and whilst so many others convert the noblest employments of human society into sordid trades, let the generous Muse resume her ancient dignity, re-assert her ancient prerogative, and instruct and reform, as well as amuse the world. Let her give a new turn to the thoughts of men, raise new affections in their minds, and determine in another and better manner the passions of their hearts. Poets, they say, were the first philosophers and divines in every country, and in ours, perhaps, the first institutions of religion and civil policy were owing to our bards. Their task might be hard, their merit was certainly great. But if they were to rise now from the dead they would find the second task, if I mistake not, much harder than the first, and confess it more easy to deal with ignorance than with error. When societies are once established and Governments formed, men flatter themselves that they proceed in cultivating the first rudiments of civility, policy, religion, and learning. But they do not observe that the private interests of many, the prejudices, affections, and passions of all, have a large share in the work, and often the largest. These put a sort of bias on the mind, which makes it decline from the straight course; and the further these supposed improvements are carried, the greater this declination grows, till men lose sight of primitive and real nature, and have no other guide but custom, a second and a false nature. The author of one is divine wisdom; of the other, human imagination; and yet whenever the second stands in opposition to the first, as it does most frequently, the second prevails. From hence it happens that the most civilised nations are often guilty of injustice and cruelty which the least civilised would abhor, and that many of the most absurd opinions and doctrines which have been imposed in the Dark Ages of ignorance continue to be the opinions and doctrines of ages enlightened by philosophy and learning. "If I was a philosopher," says Montaigne, "I would naturalise art instead of artilising Nature." The expression is odd, but the sense is good, and what he recommends would be done if the reasons that have been given did not stand in the way; if the self-interest of some men, the madness of others, and the universal pride of the human heart did not determine them to prefer error to truth and authority to reason.

Whilst your Muse is employed to lash the vicious into repentance, or to laugh the fools of the age into shame, and whilst she rises sometimes to the noblest subjects of philosophical meditation, I shall throw upon paper, for your satisfaction and for my own, some part at least of what I have thought and said formerly on the last of these subjects, as well as the reflections that they may suggest to me further in writing on them. The strange situation I am in, and the melancholy state of public affairs, take up much of my time; divide, or even dissipate, my thoughts; and, which is worse, drag the mind down by perpetual interruptions from a philosophical tone or temper to the drudgery of private and public business. The last lies nearest my heart; and since I am once more engaged in the service of my country, disarmed, gagged, and almost bound as I am, I will not abandon it as long as the integrity and perseverance of those who are under none of these disadvantages, and with whom I now co-operate, make it reasonable for me to act the same part. Further than this no shadow of duty obliges me to go. Plato ceased to act for the Commonwealth when he ceased to persuade, and Solon laid down his arms before the public magazine when Pisistratus grew too strong to be opposed any longer with hopes of success.

Though my situation and my engagements are sufficiently known to you, I choose to mention them on this occasion lest you should expect from me anything more than I find myself able to perform whilst I am in them. It has been said by many that they wanted time to make their discourses shorter; and if this be a good excuse, as I think it may be often, I lay in my claim to it. You must neither expect in what I am about to write to you that brevity which might be expected in letters or essays, nor that exactness of method, nor that fulness of the several parts which they affect to observe who presume to write philosophical treatises. The merit of brevity is relative to the manner and style in which any subject is treated, as well as to the nature of it; for the same subject may be sometimes treated very differently, and yet very properly, in both these respects. Should the poet make syllogisms in verse, or pursue a long process of reasoning in the didactic style, he would be sure to tire his reader on the whole, like Lucretius, though he reasoned better than the Roman, and put into some parts of his work the same poetical fire. He may write, as you have begun to do, on philosophical subjects, but he must write in his own character. He must contract, he may shadow, he has a right to omit whatever will not be cast in the poetic mould; and when he cannot instruct, he may hope to please. But the philosopher has no such privileges. He may contract sometimes, he must never shadow. He must be limited by his matter, lest he should grow whimsical, and by the parts of it which he understands best, lest he should grow obscure. But these parts he must develop fully, and he has no right to omit anything that may serve the purpose of truth, whether it please or not. As it would be disingenuous to sacrifice truth to popularity, so it is trifling to appeal to the reason and experience of mankind, as every philosophical writer does, or must be understood to do, and then to talk, like Plato and his ancient and modern disciples, to the imagination only. There is no need, however, to banish eloquence out of philosophy, and truth and reason are no enemies to the purity nor to the ornaments of language. But as the want of an exact determination of ideas and of an exact precision in the use of words is inexcusable in a philosopher, he must preserve them, even at the expense of style. In short, it seems to me that the business of the philosopher is to dilate, if I may borrow this word from Tully, to press, to prove, to convince; and that of the poet to hint, to touch his subject with short and spirited strokes, to warm the affections, and to speak to the heart.

Though I seem to prepare an apology for prolixity even in writing essays, I will endeavour not to be tedious, and this endeavour may succeed the better perhaps by declining any over-strict observation of method. There are certain points of that which I esteem the first philosophy whereof I shall never lose sight, but this will be very consistent with a sort of epistolary licence. To digress and to ramble are different things, and he who knows the country through which he travels may venture out of the highroad, because he is sure of finding his way back to it again. Thus the several matters that may arise even accidentally before me will have some share in guiding my pen.

I dare not promise that the sections or members of these essays will bear that nice proportion to one another and to the whole which a severe critic would require. All I dare promise you is that my thoughts, in what order soever they flow, shall be communicated to you just as they pass through my mind, just as they use to be when we converse together on these or any other subjects when we saunter alone, or, as we have often done with good Arbuthnot and the jocose Dean of St. Patrick's, among the multiplied scenes of your little garden. That theatre is large enough for my ambition. I dare not pretend to instruct mankind, and I am not humble enough to write to the public for any other purpose. I mean by writing on such subjects as I intend here, to make some trial of my progress in search of the most important truths, and to make this trial before a friend in whom I think I may confide. These epistolary essays, therefore, will be written with as little regard to form and with as little reserve as I used to show in the conversations which have given occasion to them, when I maintained the same opinions and insisted on the same reasons in defence of them.

It might seem strange to a man not well acquainted with the world, and in particular with the philosophical and theological tribe, that so much precaution should be necessary in the communication of our thoughts on any subject of the first philosophy, which is of common concern to the whole race of mankind, and wherein no one can have, according to nature and truth, any separate interest. Yet so it is. The separate interests we cannot have by God's institutions, are created by those of man; and there is no subject on which men deal more unfairly with one another than this. There are separate interests, to mention them in general only, of prejudice and of profession. By the first, men set out in the search of truth under the conduct of error, and work up their heated imaginations often to such a delirium that the more genius, and the more learning they have, the madder they grow. By the second, they are sworn, as it were, to follow all their lives the authority of some particular school, to which "tanquam scopulo, adhfrescunt;" for the condition of their engagement is to defend certain doctrines, and even mere forms of speech, without examination, or to examine only in order to defend them. By both, they become philosophers as men became Christians in the primitive Church, or as they determined themselves about disputed doctrines; for says Hilarius, writing to St. Austin, "Your holiness knows that the greatest part of the faithful embrace, or refuse to embrace, a doctrine for no reason but the impression which the name and authority of some body or other makes on them." What now can a man who seeks truth for the sake of truth, and is indifferent where he finds it, expect from any communication of his thoughts to such men as these? He will be much deceived if he expects anything better than imposition or altercation.

Few men have, I believe, consulted others, both the living and the dead, with less presumption, and in a greater spirit of docility, than I have done: and the more I have consulted, the less have I found of that inward conviction on which a mind that is not absolutely implicit can rest. I thought for a time that this must be my fault. I distrusted myself, not my teachers - men of the greatest name, ancient and modern. But I found at last that it was safer to trust myself than them, and to proceed by the light of my own understanding than to wander after these *ignes fatui* of philosophy. If I am able therefore to tell you easily, and at the same time so clearly and distinctly as to be easily understood, and so strongly as not to be easily refuted, how I have thought for myself, I shall be persuaded that I have thought enough on these subjects. If I am not able to do this, it will be evident that I have not thought on them enough. I must review my opinions, discover and correct my errors.

I have said that the subjects I mean, and which will be the principal objects of these essays, are those of the first philosophy; and it is fit, therefore, that I should explain what I understand by the first philosophy. Do not imagine that I understand what has passed commonly under that name - metaphysical pneumatics, for instance, or ontology. The first are conversant about imaginary substances, such as may and may not exist. That there is a God we can demonstrate; and although we know nothing of His manner of being, yet we acknowledge Him to be immaterial, because a thousand absurdities, and such as imply the strongest contradiction, result from the supposition that the Supreme Being is a system of matter. But of any other spirits we neither have nor can have any knowledge: and no man will be inquisitive about spiritual physiognomy, nor go about to inquire, I believe, at this time, as Evodius inquired of St. Austin, whether our immaterial part, the soul, does not remain united, when it forsakes this gross terrestrial body, to some ethereal body more subtile and more fine; which was one of the Pythagorean and Platonic whimsies: nor be under any concern to know, if this be not the case of the dead, how souls can be distinguished after their separation - that of Dives, for example, from that of Lazarus. The second - that is, ontology - treats most scientifically of being abstracted from all being ("de ente quatenus ens"). It came in fashion whilst Aristotle was in fashion, and has been spun into an immense web out of scholastic brains. But it should be, and I think it is already, left to the acute disciples of Leibnitz, who dug for gold in the ordure of the schools, and to other German wits. Let them darken by tedious definitions what is too plain to need any; or let them employ their vocabulary of barbarous terms to propagate an unintelligible jargon, which is supposed to express such abstractions as they cannot make, and according to which, however, they presume often to control the particular and most evident truths of experimental knowledge. Such reputed science deserves no rank in philosophy, not the last, and much less the first.

I desire you not to imagine neither that I understand by the first philosophy even such a science as my Lord Bacon describes - a science of general observations and axioms, such as do not belong properly to any particular part of science, but are common to many, "and of an higher stage," as he expresses himself. He complains that philosophers have not gone up to the "spring-head," which would be of "general and excellent use for the disclosing of Nature and the abridgment of art," though they "draw now and then a bucket of water out of the well for some particular use." I respect - no man more - this great authority; but I respect no authority enough to subscribe on the faith of it, to that which appears to me fantastical, as if it were real. Now this spring-head of science is purely fantastical, and the figure conveys a false notion to the mind, as figures employed licentiously are apt to do. The great author himself calls these axioms, which are to constitute his first philosophy, observations. Such they are properly; for there are some uniform principles, or uniform impressions of the same nature, to be observed in very different subjects, "una eademque naturf vestigia aut signacula diversis materiis et subjectis impressa." These observations, therefore, when they are sufficiently verified and well established, may be properly applied in discourse, or writing, from one subject to another. But I apprehend that when they are so applied, they serve rather to illustrate a proposition than to disclose Nature, or to abridge art. They may have a better foundation than similitudes and comparisons more loosely and more superficially made. They may compare realities, not appearances; things that Nature has made alike, not things that seem only to have some relation of this kind in our imaginations. But still they are comparisons of things distinct and independent. They do not lead us to things, but things that are lead us to make them. He who possesses two sciences, and the same will be often true of arts, may find in certain respects a similitude between them because he possesses both. If he did not possess both, be would be led by neither to the acquisition of the other. Such observations are effects, not means of knowledge; and, therefore, to suppose that any collection of them can constitute a science of an "higher stage," from whence we may reason `priori down to particulars, is, I presume, to suppose something very groundless, and very useless at best, to the advancement of knowledge. A pretended science of this kind must be barren of knowledge, and may be fruitful of error, as the Persian magic was, if it proceeded on the faint analogy that may be discovered between physics and politics, and deduced the rules of civil government from what the professors of it observed of the operations and works of Nature in the material world. The very specimen of their magic which my Lord Bacon has given would be sufficient to justify what is here objected to his doctrine.

Let us conclude this head by mentioning two examples among others which he brings to explain the better what he means by his first philosophy. The first is this axiom, "If to unequals you add equals, all will be unequal." This, he says, is an axiom of justice as well as of mathematics; and he asks whether there is not a true coincidence between commutative and distributive justice, and arithmetical and geometrical proportion. But I would ask in my turn whether the certainty that any arithmetician or geometrician has of the arithmetical or geometrical truth will lead him to discover this coincidence. I ask whether the most profound lawyer who never heard perhaps this axiom would be led to it by his notions of commutative and distributive justice. Certainly not. He who is well skilled in arithmetic or geometry, and in jurisprudence, may observe perhaps this uniformity of natural principle or impression because he is so skilled, though, to say the truth, it be not very obvious; but he will not have derived his knowledge of it from any spring-head of a first philosophy, from any science of an "higher stage" than arithmetic, geometry, and jurisprudence.

The second example is this axiom, "That the destruction of things is prevented by the reduction of them to their first principles." This rule is said to hold in religion, in physics, and in politics; and Machiavel is quoted for having established it in the last of these. Now though this axiom be generally, it is not universally, true; and, to say nothing of physics, it will not be hard to produce, in contradiction to it, examples of religious and civil institutions that would have perished if they had been kept strictly to their first principles, and that have been supported by departing more or less from them. It may seem justly matter of wonder that the author of the "Advancement of Learning" should espouse this maxim in religion and politics, as well as physics, so absolutely, and that he should place it as an axiom of his first philosophy relatively to the three, since he could not do it without falling into the abuse he condemns so much in his "Organum Novum" - the abuse philosophers are guilty of when they suffer the mind to rise too fast, as it is apt to do, from particulars to remote and general axioms. That the author of the "Political Discourses" should fall into this abuse is not at all strange. The same abuse runs through all his writings, in which, among many wise and many wicked reflections and precepts, he establishes frequently general maxims or rules of conduct on a few particular examples, and sometimes on a single example. Upon the whole matter, one of these axioms communicates no knowledge but that which we must have before we can know the axiom, and the other may betray us into great error when we apply it to use and action. One is unprofitable, the other dangerous; and the philosophy which admits them as principles of general knowledge deserves ill to be reputed philosophy. It would have been just as useful, and much more safe, to admit into this receptacle of axioms those self-evident and necessary truths alone of which we have an immediate perception, since they are not confined to any special parts of science, but are common to several, or to all. Thus these profitable axioms, "What is, is," "The whole is bigger than a part," and divers others, might serve to enlarge the spring-head of a first philosophy, and be of excellent use in arguing *ex præcognitis et præconcessis.*

If you ask me now what I understand then by a first philosophy, my answer will be such as I suppose you already prepared to receive. I

understand by a first philosophy, that which deserves the first place
on account of the dignity and importance of its objects, natural theology or theism, and natural religion or ethics. If we consider the
order of the sciences in their rise and progress, the first place belongs to natural philosophy, the mother of them all, or the trunk,
the tree of knowledge, out of which, and in proportion to which,
like so many branches, they all grow. These branches spread wide,
and bear even fruits of different kinds. But the sap that made them
shoot, and makes them flourish, rises from the root through the
trunk, and their productions are varied according to the variety of
strainers through which it flows. In plain terms, I speak not here of
supernatural, or revealed science; and therefore I say that all science, if it be real, must rise from below, and from our own level. It
cannot descend from above, nor from superior systems of being and
knowledge. Truth of existence is truth of knowledge, and therefore
reason searches after them in one of these scenes, where both are to
be found together, and are within our reach; whilst imagination
hopes fondly to find them in another, where both of them are to be
found, but surely not by us. The notices we receive from without
concerning the beings that surround us, and the inward conscious-
ness we have of our own, are the foundations, and the true criteri-
ons too, of all the knowledge we acquire of body and of mind: and
body and mind are objects alike of natural philosophy. We assume
commonly that they are two distinct substances. Be it so. They are
still united, and blended, as it were, together, in one human nature:
and all natures, united or not, fall within the province of natural
philosophy. On the hypothesis indeed that body and soul are two
distinct substances, one of which subsists after the dissolution of the
other, certain men, who have taken the whimsical title of metaphysicians, as if they had science beyond the bounds of Nature, or of
Nature discoverable by others, have taken likewise to themselves
the doctrine of mind; and have left that of body, under the name of
physics, to a supposed inferior order of philosophers. But the right
of these stands good; for all the knowledge that can be acquired
about mind, or the unextended substance of the Cartesians, must be
acquired, like that about body, or the extended substance, within
the bounds of their province, and by the means they employ, particular experiments and observations. Nothing can be true of mind,
any more than of body, that is repugnant to these; and an intellectu-

al hypothesis which is not supported by the intellectual phenomena is at least as ridiculous as a corporeal hypothesis which is not supported by the corporeal phenomena.

If I have said thus much in this place concerning natural philosophy, it has not been without good reason. I consider theology and ethics as the first of sciences in pre-eminence of rank. But I consider the constant contemplation of Nature - by which I mean the whole system of God's works as far as it lies open to us - as the common spring of all sciences, and even of these. What has been said agreeably to this notion seems to me evidently true; and yet metaphysical divines and philosophers proceed in direct contradiction to it, and have thereby, if I mistake not, bewildered themselves, and a great part of mankind, in such inextricable labyrinths of hypothetical reasoning, that few men can find their way back, and none can find it forward into the road of truth. To dwell long, and on some points always, in particular knowledge, tires the patience of these impetuous philosophers. They fly to generals. To consider attentively even the minutest phenomena of body and mind mortifies their pride. Rather than creep up slowly, `posteriori, to a little general knowledge, they soar at once as far and as high as imagination can carry them. From thence they descend again, armed with systems and arguments `priori; and, regardless how these agree or clash with the phenomena of Nature, they impose them on mankind.

It is this manner of philosophising, this preposterous method of beginning our search after truth out of the bounds of human knowledge, or of continuing it beyond them, that has corrupted natural theology and natural religion in all ages. They have been corrupted to such a degree that it is grown, and was so long since, as necessary to plead the cause of God, if I may use this expression after Seneca, against the divine as against the atheist; to assert his existence against the latter, to defend his attributes against the former, and to justify his providence against both. To both a sincere and humble theist might say very properly, "I make no difference between you on many occasions, because it is indifferent whether you deny or defame the Supreme Being." Nay, Plutarch, though little orthodox in theology, was not in the wrong perhaps when he declared the last to be the worst.

In treating the subjects about which I shall write to you in these letters or essays, it will be therefore necessary to distinguish genuine and pure theism from the unnatural and profane mixtures of human imagination - what we can know of God from what we cannot know. This is the more necessary, too, because, whilst true and false notions about God and religion are blended together in our minds under one specious name of science, the false are more likely to make men doubt of the true, as it often happens, than to persuade men that they are true themselves. Now, in order to this purpose, nothing can be more effectual than to go to the root of error, of that primitive error which encourages our curiosity, sustains our pride, fortifies our prejudices, and gives pretence to delusion. This primitive error consists in the high opinion we are apt to entertain of the human mind, though it holds, in truth, a very low rank in the intellectual system. To cure this error we need only turn our eyes inward, and contemplate impartially what passes there from the infancy to the maturity of the mind. Thus it will not be difficult, and thus alone it is possible, to discover the true nature of human knowledge - how far it extends, how far it is real, and where and how it begins to be fantastical.

Such an inquiry, if it cannot check the presumption nor humble the pride of metaphysicians, may serve to undeceive others. Locke pursued it; he grounded all he taught on the phenomena of Nature; he appealed to the experience and conscious knowledge of every one, and rendered all he advanced intelligible. Leibnitz, one of the vainest and most chimerical men that ever got a name in philosophy, and who is often so unintelligible that no man ought to believe he understood himself, censured Locke as a superficial philosopher. What has happened? The philosophy of one has forced its way into general approbation, that of the other has carried no conviction and scarce any information to those who have misspent their time about it. To speak the truth, though it may seem a paradox, our knowledge on many subjects, and particularly on those which we intend here, must be superficial to be real. This is the condition of humanity. We are placed, as it were, in an intellectual twilight, where we discover but few things clearly, and none entirely, and yet see just enough to tempt us with the hope of making better and more discoveries. Thus flattered, men push their inquiries on, and may be properly enough compared to Ixion, who "imagined he had Juno in his arms whilst he embraced a cloud."

To be contented to know things as God has made us capable of knowing them is, then, a first principle necessary to secure us from falling into error; and if there is any subject upon which we should be most on our guard against error, it is surely that which I have called here the first philosophy. God is hid from us in the majesty of His nature, and the little we discover of Him must be discovered by the light that is reflected from His works. Out of this light, therefore, we should never go in our inquiries and reasonings about His nature, His attributes, and the order of His providence; and yet upon these subjects men depart the furthest from it - nay, they who depart the furthest are the best heard by the bulk of mankind. The less men know, the more they believe that they know. Belief passes in their minds for knowledge, and the very circumstances which should beget doubt produce increase of faith. Every glittering apparition that is pointed out to them in the vast wild of imagination passes for a reality; and the more distant, the more confused, the more incomprehensible it is, the more sublime it is esteemed. He who should attempt to shift these scenes of airy vision for those of real knowledge might expect to be treated with scorn and anger by the whole theological and metaphysical tribe, the masters and the scholars; he would be despised as a plebeian philosopher, and railed at as an infidel. It would be sounded high that he debased human nature, which has a "cognation," so the reverend and learned Doctor Cudworth calls it, with the divine; that the soul of man, immaterial and immortal by its nature, was made to contemplate higher and nobler objects than this sensible world, and even than itself, since it was made to contemplate God and to be united to Him. In such clamour as this the voice of truth and of reason would be drowned, and, with both of them on his side, he who opposed it would make many enemies and few converts - nay, I am apt to think that some of these, if he made any, would say to him, as soon as the gaudy visions of error were dispelled, and till they were accustomed to the simplicity of truth, "Pol me occidistis." Prudence forbids me, therefore, to write as I think to the world, whilst friendship forbids me to write otherwise to you. I have been a martyr of faction in politics, and have no vocation to be so in philosophy.

But there is another consideration which deserves more regard, because it is of a public nature, and because the common interests of society may be affected by it. Truth and falsehood, knowledge and ignorance, revelations of the Creator, inventions of the creature, dictates of reason, sallies of enthusiasm, have been blended so long together in our systems of theology that it may be thought dangerous to separate them, lest by attacking some parts of these systems we should shake the whole. It may be thought that error itself deserves to be respected on this account, and that men who are deluded for their good should be deluded on.

Some such reflections as these it is probable that Erasmus made when he observed, in one of his letters to Melancthon, that Plato, dreaming of a philosophical commonwealth, saw the impossibility of governing the multitude without deceiving them. "Let not Christians lie," says this great divine: "but let it not be thought neither that every truth ought to be thrown out to the vulgar." ("Non expedit omnem veritatem prodere vulgo.") Scfvola and Varro were more explicit than Erasmus, and more reasonable than Plato. They held not only that many truths were to be concealed from the vulgar, but that it was expedient the vulgar should believe many things that were false. They distinguished at the same time, very rightly, between the regard due to religions already established, and the conduct to be held in the establishment of them. The Greek assumed that men could not be governed by truth, and erected on this principle a fabulous theology. The Romans were not of the same opinion. Varro declared expressly that if he had been to frame a new institution, he would have framed it "ex naturf potius formula." But they both thought that things evidently false might deserve an outward respect when they are interwoven into a system of government. This outward respect every good citizen will show them in such a case, and they can claim no more in any. He will not propagate these errors, but he will be cautious how he propagates even truth in opposition to them.

There has been much noise made about free-thinking; and men

have been animated in the contest by a spirit that becomes neither
the character of divines nor that of good citizens, by an arbitrary
tyrannical spirit under the mask of religious zeal, and by a
presumptuous factious spirit under that of liberty. If the first could
prevail, they would establish implicit belief and blind obedience,
and an Inquisition to maintain this abject servitude. To assert anti-
podes might become once more as heretical as Arianism or Pelagia-
nism; and men might be dragged to the jails of some Holy Office,
like Galilei, for saying they had seen what in fact they had seen, and
what every one else that pleased might see. If the second could
prevail, they would destroy at once the general influence of religion
by shaking the foundations of it which education had laid. These
are wide extremes. Is there no middle path in which a reasonable
man and a good citizen may direct his steps? I think there is.

Every one has an undoubted right to think freely - nay, it is the duty
of every one to do so as far as he has the necessary means and opportunities. This duty, too, is in no case so incumbent on him as in
those that regard what I call the first philosophy. They who have
neither means nor opportunities of this sort must submit their o-
pinions to authority; and to what authority can they resign themselves so properly and so safely as to that of the laws and constitution
of their country? In general, nothing can be more absurd than to
take opinions of the greatest moment, and such as concern us the
most intimately, on trust; but there is no help against it in many
particular cases. Things the most absurd in speculation become
necessary in practice. Such is the human constitution, and reason
excuses them on the account of this necessity. Reason does even a
little more, and it is all she can do. She gives the best direction possible to the absurdity. Thus she directs those who must believe because they cannot know, to believe in the laws of their country, and
conform their opinions and practice to those of their ancestors, to
those of Coruncanius, of Scipio, of Scfvola - not to those of Zeno, of
Cleanthes, of Chrysippus.

But now the same reason that gives this direction to such men as
these will give a very contrary direction to those who have the means and opportunities the others want. Far from advising them to
submit to this mental bondage, she will advise them to employ their

whole industry to exert the utmost freedom of thought, and to rest on no authority but hers - that is, their own. She will speak to them in the language of the Soufys, a sect of philosophers in Persia that travellers have mentioned. "Doubt," say these wise and honest freethinkers, "is the key of knowledge. He who never doubts, never examines. He who never examines, discovers nothing. He who discovers nothing, is blind and will remain so. If you find no reason to doubt concerning the opinions of your fathers, keep to them; they will be sufficient for you. If you find any reason to doubt concerning them, seek the truth quietly, but take care not to disturb the minds of other men."

Let us proceed agreeably to these maxims. Let us seek truth, but seek it quietly as well as freely. Let us not imagine, like some who are called freethinkers, that every man, who can think and judge for himself, as he has a right to do, has therefore a right of speaking, any more than of acting, according to the full freedom of his thoughts. The freedom belongs to him as a rational creature; he lies under the restraint as a member of society.

If the religion we profess contained nothing more than articles of faith and points of doctrine clearly revealed to us in the Gospel, we might be obliged to renounce our natural freedom of thought in favour of this supernatural authority. But since it is notorious that a certain order of men, who call themselves the Church, have been employed to make and propagate a theological system of their own, which they call Christianity, from the days of the Apostles, and even from these days inclusively, it is our duty to examine and analyse the whole, that we may distinguish what is divine from what is human; adhere to the first implicitly, and ascribe to the last no more authority than the word of man deserves.

Such an examination is the more necessary to be undertaken by every one who is concerned for the truth of his religion and for the honour of Christianity, because the first preachers of it were not, and they who preach it still are not, agreed about many of the most important points of their system; because the controversies raised by these men have banished union, peace, and charity out of the Christian world; and because some parts of the system savour so much of superstition and enthusiasm that all the prejudices of education and the whole weight of civil and ecclesiastical power can hardly keep them in credit. These considerations deserve the more attention because nothing can be more true than what Plutarch said of old, and my Lord Bacon has said since: one, that superstition, and the other, that vain controversies are principal causes of atheism.

I neither expect nor desire to see any public revision made of the present system of Christianity. I should fear an attempt to alter the established religion as much as they who have the most bigot attachment to it, and for reasons as good as theirs, though not entirely the same. I speak only of the duty of every private man to examine for himself, which would have an immediate good effect relatively to himself, and might have in time a good effect relatively to the public, since it would dispose the minds of men to a greater indifference about theological disputes, which are the disgrace of Christianity and have been the plagues of the world.

Will you tell me that private judgment must submit to the established authority of Fathers and Councils? My answer shall be that the Fathers, ancient and modern, in Councils and out of them, have raised that immense system of artificial theology by which genuine Christianity is perverted and in which it is lost. These Fathers are fathers of the worst sort, such as contrive to keep their children in a perpetual state of infancy, that they may exercise perpetual and absolute dominion over them. "Quo magis regnum in illos exerceant pro sua libidine." I call their theology artificial, because it is in a multitude of instances conformable neither to the religion of Nature nor to Gospel Christianity, but often repugnant to both, though said to be founded on them. I shall have occasion to mention several such instances in the course of these little essays. Here I will only observe that if it be hard to conceive how anything so absurd as the pagan theology stands represented by the Fathers who wrote against it, and as it really was, could ever gain credit among rational creatures, it is full as hard to conceive how the artificial theology we speak of could ever prevail, not only in ages of ignorance, but in the most enlightened. There is a letter of St. Austin wherein he says that he was ashamed of himself when he refuted the opinions of the former, and that he was ashamed of mankind when he considered that such absurdities were received and defended. The reflections might be retorted on the saint, since he broached and defended doctrines as unworthy of the Supreme All-Perfect Being as those which the heathens taught concerning their fictitious and inferior gods. Is it necessary to quote any other than that by which we are taught that God has created numbers of men for no purpose but to damn them? "Quisquis prfdestinationis doctrinam invidia gravat," says Calvin, "aperte maledicit Deo." Let us say, "Quisquis prfdestinationis doctrinam asserit, blasphemat". Let us not impute such cruel injustice to the all-perfect Being. Let Austin and Calvin and all those who teach it be answerable for it alone. You may bring Fathers and Councils as evidences in the cause of artificial theology, but reason must be the judge; and all I contend for is, that she should be so in the breast of every Christian that can appeal to her tribunal.

Will you tell me that even such a private examination of the Christian system as I propose that every man who is able to make it should make for himself, is unlawful; and that, if any doubts arise in our minds concerning religion, we must have recourse for the solution of them to some of that holy order which was instituted, by God Himself, and which has been continued by the imposition of hands in every Christian society, from the Apostles down to the present clergy? My answer shall be shortly this: it is repugnant to all the ideas of wisdom and goodness to believe that the universal terms of salvation are knowable by the means of one order of men alone, and that they continue to be so even after they have been published to all nations. Some of your directors will tell you that whilst Christ was on earth the Apostles were the Church; that He was the Bishop of it; that afterwards the admission of men into this order was approved, and confirmed by visions and other divine manifestations; and that these wonderful proofs of God's interposition at the ordinations and consecrations of presbyters and bishops lasted even in the time of St. Cyprian - that is, in the middle of the third century. It is pity that they lasted no longer, for the honour of the Church, and for the conviction of those who do not sufficiently reverence the religious society. It were to be wished, perhaps, that some of the secrets of electricity were improved enough to be piously and usefully applied to this purpose. If we beheld a shekinah, or divine presence, like the flame of a taper, on the heads of those who receive the imposition of hands, we might believe that they receive the Holy Ghost at the same time. But as we have no reason to believe what superstitious, credulous, or lying men (such as Cyprian himself was) reported formerly, that they might establish the proud pretensions of the clergy, so we have no reason to believe that five men of this order have any more of the Divine Spirit in our time, after they are ordained, than they had before. It would be a farce to provoke laughter, if there was no suspicion of profanation in it, to see them gravely lay hands on one another, and bid one another receive the Holy Ghost.

Will you tell me finally, in opposition to what has been said, and that you may anticipate what remains to be said, that laymen are not only unauthorised, but quite unequal, without the assistance of divines, to the task I propose? If you do, I shall make no scruple to tell you, in return, that laymen may be, if they please, in every respect as fit, and are in one important respect more fit than divines to go through this examination, and to judge for themselves upon it. We say that the Scriptures, concerning the divine authenticity of which all the professors of Christianity agree, are the sole criterion of Christianity. You add tradition, concerning which there may be, and there is, much dispute. We have, then, a certain invariable rule whenever the Scriptures speak plainly. Whenever they do not speak so, we have this comfortable assurance - that doctrines which nobody understands are revealed to nobody, and are therefore improper objects of human inquiry. We know, too, that if we receive the explanations and commentaries of these dark sayings from the clergy, we take the greatest part of our religion from the word of man, not from the Word of God. Tradition, indeed, however derived, is not to be totally rejected; for if it was, how came the canon of the Scriptures, even of the Gospels, to be fixed? How was it conveyed down to us? Traditions of general facts, and general propositions plain and uniform, may be of some authority and use. But particular anecdotical traditions, whose original authority is unknown, or justly suspicious, and that have acquired only an appearance of generality and notoriety, because they have been frequently and boldly repeated from age to age, deserve no more regard than doctrines evidently added to the Scriptures, under pretence of explaining and

commenting them, by men as fallible as ourselves. We may receive
the Scriptures, and be persuaded of their authenticity, on the faith of
ecclesiastical tradition; but it seems to me that we may reject, at the
same time, all the artificial theology which has been raised on these
Scriptures by doctors of the Church, with as much right as they
receive the Old Testament on the authority of Jewish scribes and
doctors whilst they reject the oral law and all rabbinical literature.

He who examines on such principles as these, which are conformable to truth and reason, may lay aside at once the immense volumes
of Fathers and Councils, of schoolmen, casuists, and controversial
writers, which have perplexed the world so long. Natural religion
will be to such a man no longer intricate, revealed religion will be
no longer mysterious, nor the Word of God equivocal. Clearness
and precision are two great excellences of human laws. How much
more should we expect to find them in the law of God? They have
been banished from thence by artificial theology, and he who is
desirous to find them must banish the professors of it from his
councils, instead of consulting them. He must seek for genuine
Christianity with that simplicity of spirit with which it is taught in
the Gospel by Christ Himself. He must do the very reverse of what
has been done by the persons you advise him to consult.

You see that I have said what has been said, on a supposition that,
however obscure theology may be, the Christian religion is extremely plain, and requires no great learning nor deep meditation to
develop it. But if it was not so plain, if both these were necessary to
develop it, is great learning the monopoly of the clergy since the
resurrection of letters, as a little learning was before that era? Is
deep meditation and justness of reasoning confined to men of that
order by a peculiar and exclusive privilege? In short, and to ask a
question which experience will decide, have these men who boast
that they are appointed by God "to be the interpreters of His secret
will, to represent His person, and to answer in His name, as it were,
out of the sanctuary" - have these men, I say, been able in more than
seventeen centuries to establish an uniform system of revealed religion - for natural religion never wanted their help among the civil
societies of Christians - or even in their own? They do not seem to
have aimed at this desirable end. Divided as they have always been,

they have always studied in order to believe, and to take upon trust, or to find matter of discourse, or to contradict and confute, but never to consider impartially nor to use a free judgment. On the contrary, they who have attempted to use this freedom of judgment have been constantly and cruelly persecuted by them.

The first steps towards the establishment of artificial theology, which has passed for Christianity ever since, were enthusiastical. They were not heretics alone who delighted in wild allegories and the pompous jargon of mystery; they were the orthodox Fathers of the first ages, they were the disciples of the Apostles, or the scholars of their disciples; for the truth of which I may appeal to the epistles and other writings of these men that are extant - to those of Clemens, of Ignatius, or of Irenfus, for instance - and to the visions of Hermes, that have so near a resemblance to the productions of Bunyan.

The next steps of the same kind were rhetorical. They were made by men who declaimed much and reasoned ill, but who imposed on the imaginations of others by the heat of their own, by their hyperboles, their exaggerations, the acrimony of their style, and their violent invectives. Such were the Chrysostoms, the Jeromes, an Hilarius, a Cyril, and most of the Fathers.

The last of the steps I shall mention were logical, and these were made very opportunely and very advantageously for the Church and for artificial theology. Absurdity in speculation and superstition in practice had been cultivated so long, and were become so gross, that men began to see through the veils that had been thrown over them, as ignorant as those ages were. Then the schoolmen arose. I need not display their character; it is enough known. This only I will say - that having very few materials of knowledge and much subtilty of wit they wrought up systems of fancy on the little they knew, and invented an art, by the help of Aristotle, not of enlarging, but of puzzling, knowledge with technical terms, with definitions, distinctions, and syllogisms merely verbal. They taught what they could not explain, evaded what they could not answer, and he who had the most skill in this art might put to silence, when it came into general use, the man who was consciously certain that he had truth and reason on his side.

The authority of the schools lasted till the resurrection of letters. But as soon as real knowledge was enlarged, and the conduct of the understanding better understood, it fell into contempt. The advocates of artificial theology have had since that time a very hard task. They have been obliged to defend in the light what was imposed in the dark, and to acquire knowledge to justify ignorance. They were drawn to it with reluctance. But learning, that grew up among the laity, and controversies with one another, made this unavoidable, which was not eligible on the principles of ecclesiastical policy. They have done with these new arms all that great parts, great pains, and great zeal could do under such disadvantages, and we may apply to this order, on this occasion, "si Pergama dextra," etc. But their Troy cannot be defended; irreparable breaches have been made in it. They have improved in learning and knowledge, but this improvement has been general, and as remarkable at least among the laity as among the clergy. Besides which it must be owned that the former have had in this respect a sort of indirect obligation to the latter; for whilst these men have searched into antiquity, have improved criticism, and almost exhausted subtilty, they have furnished so many arms the more to such of the others as do not submit implicitly to them, but examine and judge for themselves. By refuting one another, when they differ, they have made it no hard matter to refute them all when they agree. And I believe there are few books written to propagate or defend the received notions of artificial theology which may not be refuted by the books themselves. I conclude, on the whole, that laymen have, or need to have, no want of the clergy in examining and analysing the religion they profess.

But I said that they are in one important respect more fit to go through this examination without the help of divines than with it. A layman who seeks the truth may fall into error; but as he can have no interest to deceive himself, so he has none of profession to bias his private judgment, any more than to engage him to deceive others. Now, the clergyman lies strongly under this influence in every communion. How, indeed, should it be otherwise? Theology is become one of those sciences which Seneca calls "scientif in lucrum exeuntes;" and sciences, like arts whose object is gain, are, in good English, trades. Such theology is, and men who could make no fortune, except the lowest, in any other, make often the highest in this; for the proof of which assertion I might produce some signal instances among my lords the bishops. The consequence has been uniform; for how ready soever the tradesmen of one Church are to expose the false wares - that is, the errors and abuses - of another, they never admit that there are any in their own; and he who admitted this in some particular instance would be driven out of the ecclesiastical company as a false brother and one who spoiled the trade.

Thus it comes to pass that new Churches may be established by the dissensions, but that old ones cannot be reformed by the concurrence, of the clergy. There is no composition to be made with this order of men. He who does not believe all they teach in every communion is reputed nearly as criminal as he who believes no part of it. He who cannot assent to the Athanasian Creed, of which Archbishop Tillotson said, as I have heard, that he wished we were well rid, would receive no better quarter than an atheist from the generality of the clergy. What recourse now has a man who cannot be thus implicit? Some have run into scepticism, some into atheism, and, for fear of being imposed on by others, have imposed on themselves. The way to avoid these extremes is that which has been chalked out in this introduction. We may think freely without thinking as licentiously as divines do when they raise a system of imagination on true foundations, or as sceptics do when they renounce all knowledge, or as atheists do when they attempt to demolish the foundations of all religion and reject demonstration. As we think for ourselves, we may keep our thoughts to ourselves, or communicate them with a due reserve and in such a manner only as it may be done without offending the laws of our country and disturbing the public peace.

I cannot conclude my discourse on this occasion better than by putting you in mind of a passage you quoted to me once, with great applause, from a sermon of Foster, and to this effect: "Where mystery begins, religion ends." The apophthegm pleased me much, and I was glad to hear such a truth from any pulpit, since it shows an inclination, at least, to purify Christianity from the leaven of artificial theology, which consists principally in making things that are very plain mysterious, and in pretending to make things that are impenetrably mysterious very plain. If you continue still of the same mind, I shall have no excuse to make to you for what I have written and shall write. Our opinions coincide. If you have changed your mind, think again and examine further. You will find that it is the modest, not the presumptuous, inquirer who makes a real and safe progress in the discovery of divine truths. One follows Nature and Nature's God - that is, he follows God in His works and in His Word; nor presumes to go further, by metaphysical and theological commentaries of his own invention, than the two texts, if I may use this expression, carry him very evidently. They who have done otherwise, and have affected to discover, by a supposed science derived from tradition or taught in the schools, more than they who have not such science can discover concerning the nature, physical and moral, of the Supreme Being, and concerning the secrets of His providence, have been either enthusiasts or knaves, or else of that numerous tribe who reason well very often, but reason always on some arbitrary supposition.

Much of this character belonged to the heathen divines, and it is in all its parts peculiarly that of the ancient Fathers and modern doctors of the Christian Church. The former had reason, but no revelation, to guide them; and though reason be always one, we cannot wonder that different prejudices and different tempers of imagination warped it in them on such subjects as these, and produced all the extravagances of their theology. The latter had not the excuse of human frailty to make in mitigation of their presumption. On the contrary, the consideration of this frailty, inseparable from their nature, aggravated their presumption. They had a much surer criterion than human reason; they had divine reason and the Word of God to guide them and to limit their inquiries. How came they to go beyond this criterion? Many of the first preachers were led into it because they preached or wrote before there was any such criterion established, in the acceptance of which they all agreed, because they preached or wrote, in the meantime, on the faith of tradition and on a confidence that they were persons extraordinarily gifted. Other reasons succeeded these. Skill in languages, not the gift of tongues,

some knowledge of the Jewish cabala and some of heathen philosophy, of Plato's especially, made them presume to comment, and
under that pretence to enlarge the system of Christianity with as
much licence as they could have taken if the word of man, instead
of the Word of God, had been concerned, and they had commented
the civil, not the divine, law. They did this so copiously that, to give
one instance of it, the exposition of St. Matthew's Gospel took up
ninety homilies, and that of St. John's eighty-seven, in the works of
Chrysostom; which puts me in mind of a Puritanical parson who, if
I mistake not - for I have never looked into the folio since I was a
boy and condemned sometimes to read in it - made one hundred
and nineteen sermons on the hundred and nineteenth Psalm.

Now all these men, both heathens and Christians, appeared gigantic
forms through the false medium of imagination and habitual prejudice; but were, in truth, as arrant dwarfs in the knowledge to which
they pretended as you and I and all the sons of Adam. The former,
however, deserved some excuse; the latter none. The former made a
very ill use of their reason, no doubt, when they presume to dogma-
tise about the divine nature, but they deceived nobody. What they
taught, they taught on their own authority, which every other man
was at liberty to receive or reject as he approved or disapproved the
doctrine. Christians, on the other hand, made a very ill use of revelation and reason both. Instead of employing the superior principle to direct and confine the inferior, they employed it to sanctify
all that wild imagination, the passions, and the interests of the
ecclesiastical order suggested. This abuse of revelation was so scandalous that whilst they were building up a system of religion under
the name of Christianity, every one who sought to signalise himself
in the enterprise - and they were multitudes - dragged the Scriptures to his opinion by different interpretations, paraphrases, com-
ments. Arius and Nestorius both pretended that they had it on their
sides; Athanasius and Cyril on theirs. They rendered the Word of
God so dubious that it ceased to be a criterion, and they had recourse to another - to Councils and the decrees of Councils. He must be
very ignorant in ecclesiastical antiquity who does not know by what
intrigues of the contending factions - for such they were, and of the
worst kind - these decrees were obtained; and yet, an opinion
prevailing that the Holy Ghost, the same Divine Spirit who dictated

the Scriptures, presided in these assemblies and dictated their decrees, their decrees passed for infallible decisions, and sanctified,
little by little, much of the superstition, the nonsense, and even the
blasphemy which the Fathers taught, and all the usurpations of the
Church. This opinion prevailed and influenced the minds of men so
powerfully and so long that Erasmus, who owns in one of his letters
that the writings of Œcolampadius against transubstantiation seemed sufficient to seduce even the elect ("ut seduci posse videantur
etiam electi"), declares in another that nothing hindered him from
embracing the doctrine of Œcolampadius but the consent of the
Church to the other doctrine ("nisi obstaret consensus Ecclesif").
Thus artificial theology rose on the demolitions, not on the foundations, of Christianity; was incorporated into it; and became a principal part of it. How much it becomes a good Christian to distinguish
them, in his private thoughts at least, and how unfit even the greatest, the most moderate, and the least ambitious of the ecclesiastical
order are to assist us in making this distinction, I have endeavoured
to show you by reason and by example.

It remains, then, that we apply ourselves to the study of the first
philosophy without any other guides than the works and the Word
of God. In natural religion the clergy are unnecessary; in revealed
they are dangerous guides.